KT-483-862

Derek Tangye has become famous all over the world for his series of best sellers about his flower farm in Cornwall. The series, which began with *A Gull on the Roof*, describes a simple way of life which thousands of his readers would like to adopt themselves.

Derek and his wife left their glamorous existence in London when they discovered Minack, a deserted cottage close to the cliffs of Mount's Bay. Jeannie gave up her job as Press Relations Officer of the Savoy Hotel Group and Derek Tangye resigned from M.I.5. They then proceeded to carve from the wild land around the cottage the meadows which became their flower farm.

Also by Derek Tangye and available from Sphere Books

COTTAGE ON A CLIFF
THE WAY TO MINACK

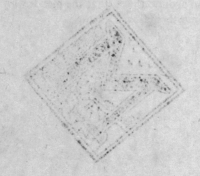

A Cat Affair

DEREK TANGYE

SPHERE BOOKS LIMITED
30/32 Gray's Inn Road, London WC1X 8JL

First published in Great Britain by Michael Joseph Ltd 1974
Copyright © Derek Tangye 1974
Published by Sphere Books 1976
Reprinted 1976, 1977, 1978, 1979
The illustrations in the hardback edition have been omitted

For Jeannie

Set in Linotype Pilgrim

Printed in Great Britain by
Hunt Barnard Printing Ltd, Aylesbury, Bucks.

ONE

'What are you looking at?' Jeannie asked.

A warm, late October afternoon, and we had taken our saucerless cups of tea to the terrace close to the cottage we call the bridge, a convenient name for a corner of Minack where there was a spreading view of the moorlands, the sea, and the curving line of the Lizard; and where Jeannie and I often sat or stood watching, absorbing the antics of birds, or a fox, or the changing colours of light, or the passing of the seasons, green bracken, brown bracken, flattened bracken, wasting time by watching.

'There's something black in the corner of Bill's field,' I said, 'over by the hedge on the right. I thought it was a carrion crow at first . . .'

'What is it then?'

'I need my field glasses.'

'I'll fetch them.'

Jeannie ran back to the door of the cottage, passing Lama curled like a black cushion in the cup of an old rock, one of the rocks which formed the foundation of the cottage. A rock which had been there since the beginning of time, solid witness of history . . . Athelstan, Middle Ages, the Spanish Armada, Marlborough, the loss of the American Colonies, the Bastille, the Prince Regent and Beau Brummel, Trafalgar, William the Fourth and the Reform Bill, Melbourne, youthful Queen Victoria falling in love with Albert, the unorganised emotions of the Brontës, the Great Exhibition, Oscar Wilde, Mafeking, Edwardian grace, Bleriot, Passchendael, Marconi's first message across the Atlantic, horses leaving the land, old values fading, jumbo jets pencilling the sky, ocean liners discarded, cement, motorways, over-population . . . the rock where Lama curled was the same as in the beginning.

'Here they are.'

I had not possessed these glasses for long, yet the varnish had been scratched off the rims so that they appeared to be uncared-for glasses; and although I had not been responsible for this myself, my forgetfulness had caused it to happen. Soon after I had bought them Jeannie and I had taken a walk along the cliffs with Penny and Fred the donkeys.

Penny had come into our lives as a result of a visit we made one early summer evening to a pub called the Plume of Feathers at Scorrier near Redruth. It was intended to be a normal, casual visit, a drink or two and then away. But as I was enjoying my drink, the landlord who was also a horse dealer led Jennie out of the pub to a field at the back where a forlorn, black donkey with a patchy coat, and spread-eagled feet due to lack of farrier attention, stood alone by a hedge. It was a cunning move on the part of the landlord. He was wanting to make a sale, and he immediately suc-ceeded in snaring Jeannie into becoming an emotional ally.

An hour later a sale was completed, and instead of return-ing home on our own we had a donkey in the back of the Land Rover; and the donkey, as if to display her gratitude, spent the journey with her head gently resting on my shoulder as I drove. I was flattered, but not happy. I had no knowledge of donkeys. I even half expected that she might suddenly bite me. I did not share the life-long love of donkeys that Jeannie had always enjoyed. I was suspicious of them. And when a month later Penny, as we now called her, gave birth to Fred, I found myself reflecting that the visit to the Plume of Feathers was the oddest visit to a pub I had ever made.

I have not, however, regretted it. The setting of Minack suits the presence of donkeys. Minack lies over a mile off the road that leads to Sparnon, Poljigga and Land's End, along a winding, hedge-enclosed lane which scares city-accustomed motorists into fearing their cars will be damaged by the bumpy surface; then past a huddle of farm buildings, and downwards towards the sea and the cottage. We now have twenty acres, all rented from a big Cornish landowner, and the fields and the meadows fall down towards the sea's edge. We grow daffodils for the early spring market, and tomatoes in greenhouses during the summer; and though these crops take up much of the land there is plenty to spare where the donkeys can roam. Once upon a time we used to allow them to wander in the little wood which edges the cottage, but they developed a taste for the bark of the elm trees, ripping it off in strips and eating it; and so they are now banned from the wood. They are banned too, of course, from the daffodil meadows as soon as the green spikes poke from the soil in early December, though when the bulbs are dormant they often meander from meadow to meadow; and sometimes we will come across them in a meadow close to the sea. It is a handsome sight, two donkeys silhouetted against grey rocks and the sea.

But they also demand diversions; and one of these diversions is the walk along the cliffs towards Lamorna, the straggling village in a steep valley, with a small harbour for fishing boats, and a bay which on summer days reminds me of a lagoon I once knew on the island of Moorea near Tahiti. The path we walk along is a narrow one with gorse bushes on either side, and brambles, and waist-high bracken; and there would be no path at all had we not ourselves kept it open, periodically through the year cutting the undergrowth back so that there is always a path, although a rough one. We walk in single file, no halters on the donkeys; and because we always take this walk early in the morning, we seldom meet anyone on the way.

We saw no one, for that matter, on the morning I lost my field glasses. We had not gone far, just over the Minack boundary hedge and on towards the headland of Carn Barges, when we paused to watch the *Stella*, the Trinity House vessel, pass by a mile or so off-shore sailing west towards the Wolf Rock. Nothing unusual about that. We often have watched her; and the watching is only because we live a life which lends itself to watching. We have time to watch. On this occasion I also had time to forget . . . for after gazing at the *Stella* through my field glasses, I put them down on a boulder siding the path; and I did not realise I had done so until I reached a point above the bay of Lamorna where we always paused in our walk, letting the donkeys dally among the grasses of the area which they seemed particularly to enjoy. Then I saw a crabber below us, and the man was pulling in his pots, and I wanted to see what he had caught. It was at this moment I found I had left my field glasses behind.

'Damn,' I said.

'Nobody's around,' said Jeannie, 'they'll be there when we get back.'

They were not.

In such a situation one immediately has doubts. Did I leave them on that boulder, or did I put them down in the bracken, or under one of the elderberry trees? We scavenged among the undergrowth, and found no glasses. Then I wondered if some hiker had found them, then walked the few hundred yards to the cottage to announce his discovery. But when we returned to the cottage, Geoffrey was there . . . Geoffrey, who for some years has been our aide at Minack; and he had seen no one.

By this time fog had begun to come in from the sea; and I realised that if a hiker had taken the glasses, it would be no use trying to follow him towards Lands End, for the simple reason I would not be able to see him. So I gave up the search, annoyed with myself for having been so vague; and wondering what I should do next. I did nothing until the following day when the weather had cleared; and then I proceeded on a line of detective work which was to have a surprising result.

On the boundary path between Minack and the neighbouring property is a Trinity House notice warning the public to keep away from the unmanned lighthouse several

8

hundred yards away down the bottom of the cliff. The notice, however, is ambiguous; and many a stranger who reads it concludes that Trinity House is banning him from walking any further. This naturally causes irritation; and I sometimes have met frustrated hikers who were in high dudgeon over this apparent denial of free walking. I thereupon explain that the offending notice is meant only to apply to the land in the immediate neighbourhood of the lighthouse; and adding my own opinion that Trinity House should be forced to remove the notice to the point concerned.

The notice, painted black against the white of the board, was therefore contentious; and yet I had never seen rude remarks scribbled upon it until the morning I began to search for the person who had taken my glasses. Then, on coming to the noticeboard, I by chance observed that a message *had* been written on it; and it must have been written recently because I had passed that way only a couple of days previously. The message read: 'A curse upon those who deny me entry.' And it was signed. The name was Brown.

I naturally had sympathy for Mr Brown; and apart from the annoyance caused by the notice I was also occasionally vexed by unnecessary sounding of the lighthouse fog signal. The signal was controlled by remote control. Somebody would report fog several miles away to the duty officer at the Penzance Trinity House depot . . . and he would promptly press a button for our fog signal to sound. It was of no matter that the weather in our area was horizon clear.

I was, however, on this occasion grateful to Trinity House and the noticeboard for providing me with a clue. Anyone, I reckoned, who wrote such a positive message on a lonely Cornish cliff at a time of year when normal holidaymakers were back at their offices, was also capable of taking a pair of field glasses he might find on a boulder. I had a further hunch. He was obviously a stranger, otherwise he would have brought the glasses to the cottage after he had found them; and as he was a stranger he was most likely to be on a walking tour . . . and, this was my hunch, he would be staying at night at the Cornish Youth Hostels.

Such a hostel was situated in lovely Cot Valley not far from St Just; and it would be this hostel that Mr Brown would have aimed for on the day he wrote his defiant message. As it happened some event diverted me from following up my hunch for a couple of days, but when I did so my hunch was proved to be correct. A Mr Brown *had* stayed there on the night in question. He had never mentioned he had found any field glasses, nor had the warden seen him with a pair. But his stay was short, and he was off again in the morning after leaving his address in the visitors' book which the warden was good enough to give me.

It was a North Country address, and I received no reply after writing to it. Weeks went by, and I heard nothing. Then I wrote again saying that unless I received a reply within a week I would put the matter into the hands of the police. I was still, remember, working on a hunch. Only the hunch, the unreasonable, illogical hunch, prompted the thought that Mr Brown was the culprit.

And he was. One morning the postman brought me a parcel, and the tired-looking, varnish-bare field glasses were in it. So too was a note, and a new address. The address was that of an officer cadet training unit, and the note one of apology. A mild apology. Should I have written to the CO of the training unit to tell him that one of his cadets would have been guilty of stealing unless I had called his bluff? I didn't. Nor did I write to Mr Brown. I did, however, write to my insurance company which by now had accepted my claim that my field glasses had been lost, and returned the money they had sent me. But what of Mr Brown? I wonder if he still remembers his walk along Minack cliffs.

I now looked across the narrow valley to Bill's field and to what I thought for a moment to be a carrion crow; and I now saw clearly that I was watching a black cat.

'A black cat,' I said to Jeannie, 'which is about to jump.'

Its body was quivering, paws were shuffling to gain the feel of a comfortable springboard, a mouse was about to be its victim, then a leap . . . and failure. Too soon or too late I would never know, because all I could see was a spread-eagled posterior, and obvious frustration.

'Let *me* have a look,' said Jeannie, and I handed her the glasses.

'He's pretending it never happened. He's found a tuft of grass to be interested in.'

At that moment, if I had known it, the step had been taken that was to change our life at Minack.

And that of Lama.

The black cat over there by the hedge had begun his campaign to return to Minack.

TWO

I saw Lama for the first time also at a distance. It was early
March, twelve years before; and I watched her slipping
along between the daffodil beds one morning, then a few
days later I saw her again, crouched in the meadow where
we grew calendulas, a tussock of black among the red-
gold of the flowers. I thought nothing of her. Just a wild
black cat which happened to be around. It would go. It
would leave as soon as it tired of Minack as a hunting
ground. A wild cat is like a fox, or a hawk, or an owl, roaming an area for a while as if it owned it, then away to other
country.

I had, in any case, the matter of the flower season to think
about. My mind becomes one-track during the flower season
. . . letters are unanswered, bills unpaid, visitors hurried
away, and any diversions ignored. Today we specialise in
growing a sequence of early daffodils, Magnificence, Joseph
McLeod, Hollywood, Dutchmaster, California and others;
and for six weeks they dominate our lives. Every day
we race them to the London market cursing when the
weather is warm thus forcing the buds to burst too quickly,
cursing also the glasshouse, up-country daffodils which now
often clash with our open-grown blooms so causing a glut;
and then occasionally rejoicing when we open the post and
find the prices for the preceding day are unexpectedly good.
It is a hectic period of picking, bunching, packing, and rushing the boxes to catch the afternoon flower train at
Penzance.

But at the time I first saw Lama, we grew many other

kinds of flowers as well. We grew freesias in a greenhouse, and several thousand Bournemouth Gem violet plants, and meadows of winter flowering wallflowers, Beauty of Nice stocks, De Caen anemones, calendulas, and forget-me-nots. Our flower season in those days began in October and continued through the winter months to the end of March; and we had helping us two girls, Jane and Shelagh; and Geoffrey Semmens who is still with us.

Jane left to go to live in the Scilly Islands, and she is there now with a home on Tresco for her two children and Dick her husband, a brilliant model maker in wood, who also works in the famous Tresco Gardens. Shelagh is dead. She died a week after her twentieth birthday, suddenly. Jeannie had given her for that birthday a white frilly blouse, and I remember Shelagh's excitement after she had undone the gaily coloured parcel, saying that she would wear it on some special occasion in a fortnight's time. But of course she never wore it. She had a weak heart that nobody knew about, and she had an attack one morning when she was bicycling to Minack; and at the very moment she died I still swear I heard the sound of her bicycle wheels on the gravel outside our bedroom window. 'Shelagh has arrived,' I said to Jeannie at the time, 'she's putting her bike away.'

These two, Shelagh and Jane, while they were with us gave us much happiness, for they had the gift of enthusiasm; and they had a love for the flowers, the bunching and the boxing and the picking, which had no connection with their pay packets. They had pride in the outcome of what they did. At a time when there were many financial anxieties for Jeannie and myself they made it easier for us to face these anxieties. They also made it easier for Jeannie to court the little black cat I had first seen between the daffodil beds, then later in the calendula meadow. For they were to be her allies; and I to be the odd one out.

The truth is, of course, that I was brought up to dislike cats. My mother and father were dog people, and so my youth was spent loving an old English sheepdog called Lance, and another called Roy; and there was a white coated mongrel called Bruce who saw me off from Glendorgal, our family home on the north coast of Cornwall, when I left for my first term at Copthorne, a preparatory school. And there were the Maltese terriers which my mother loved: Mary, then Gay, then Pickles. I left all these tearfully at the end of holidays, rushed to them happily at the beginning of others. But there were no cats. Cats, in my family, were considered vermin. I have a suspicion that I now know why. My family was a law abiding one . . . dogs had licences, cats were spared them. A dog, therefore, was the superior animal. Cats were the poor whites of the community.

This attitude towards cats was ingrained in me until I met Jeannie; and a long time after for that matter. Courtship is not easy if one party is strongly averse to the behaviour of the other in some respect; and I frequently expressed my opinion that her dotty attitude towards cats was unattractive. I found, for instance, as she and I were sauntering arm in arm down some London street that she would suddenly break away from me, dash across the street . . . and all because she had seen some mangy tabby whose morale, she thought, would benefit from her attention.

Then the day came when I was to be introduced to her parents, and I set off to their large house on a hill in St Albans in apprehensive mood. They gave me, however, a warm welcome, led me into the drawing room and offered me a cup of tea. I placed the cup on a small table beside my chair, and sat down, Jeannie watching me from the other side of the room. It was at this moment that Tim, the large Blue Persian of the house, stalked into the room, advanced towards me unnoticed, then jumped on to my lap. The serenity of the occasion was immediately broken. I found myself automatically seizing this specimen of vermin, and flinging it away from me. Unhappily I flung it the wrong way. I flung it towards the small table beside me where stood my cup of tea; and a few seconds later I was on my hands and knees mopping up the contents with my handkerchief, apologising profusely to my future in-laws.

After our marriage Jeannie took positive steps to change

me from being an anti-cat man; and one afternoon I went into her office at the Savoy and found her secretary playing with a small ginger kitten. It had already been named. The Eighth Army had just broken through at El Alamein, and the kitten had been given the name of the victor . . . Monty. It had also been given an assured home; for I took it back that evening to our house overlooking the Thames at Mortlake. Monty was there for seven years, then at Minack for another eight; and by the time he died, he had become for me as close a friend as any Old English sheepdog I knew as a child. He was the recipient of my secret thoughts. A reliable anchor. He had even veered me towards appreciating the charms of his race.

But not quite. When he died, it was inconceivable for me to replace him casually by another. I was still immune from general cat charm. I remember when we first came to Minack there was a grey and white cat which hovered in the neighbourhood of the cottage; and one paw was missing, victim of a gin trap no doubt, and it looked appealingly at me as if it was saying: 'So you have come to this empty cottage . . . please let me belong to it,' Such a heart-rending situation could easily have seduced Jeannie. Not me. I shooed the cat away. Monty was the new owner of Minack, and I would not let him have any competition. Mind you, I have thought of that three-legged cat many times since.

So when Monty died, I covered my grief by saying that I would never have another cat. But having said that, I added a remark to Jeannie which had mystical results. I said that the only cat I would have again had to be black, had to come to the cottage in a storm, and that we would never be able to trace the home it came from. True, I had always believed in the luck of black cats even in my most virulent anti-cat period. But it seemed to be expecting too much for such conditions ever to be realised.

They were . . . though they were egged on by the plotting of Jeannie, Jane and Shelagh.

Throughout that flower season my one-track mind was interrupted from time to time by the sight of saucers in strange places. Beside the little stream at the entrance to Minack which we called Monty's Leap. On the stone wall in sight of the shed where we bunched the flowers. Often much further away. Thus I would stumble on an empty saucer in the wallflower meadow, or on the path to the onion meadow. These saucers, it slowly dawned on me, were my enemies. Jeannie, Jane and Shelagh had decided that it was time to replace Monty. The little black cat was at hand, roaming the area; and so why not help to make up its mind to live at Minack by tempting it with milk and food?

'This is simply not good enough,' I said to them severely as we stood all together at the bench bunching anemones, 'I don't want any cat to be encouraged to come here.'

'But it's starving,' said Jane.

'I threw it chicken pellets this morning,' said Shelagh, 'and they fell among the gravel and the cat pecked them out like a bird.'

'You remember what you promised,' said Jeannie.

'It wasn't a promise,' I replied defensively.

Of course it wasn't a promise. I had stipulated impossible conditions. The cat might one day be *bribed* by the three of them to want to live at Minack, but there was nothing for me to fear in that. I would unhesitatingly bar its presence, throw water at it, shoo it away. I had made no promise, unless the impossible conditions were fulfilled.

I kept my word.

On Easter Sunday a south-easterly gale blew all day and into the night, roaring round the cottage so that we were enclosed by its noise. But above it all, just as we were going to bed, I suddenly heard a cry at the door, like the squeak of maladjusted car brakes . . . and when I opened the door, holding it against the wind, in rushed the little black cat.

'Extraordinary,' I said doubtfully, realising my independence was about to end, realising that my legs would soon be having cramp again as I lay in bed, realising that I would soon be making trivial sacrifices for the cat's benefit, realising that I would never be able to go away without the nagging concern of: 'Who will look after the cat?'

Nevertheless I still had an escape route. I had also stipulated that the black cat, which might come to the cottage door in a storm, should have no previous home. Supposing someone was grieving for this one? Supposing it had wandered afar and become lost? How happy would be the owners, and myself, if I could find them!

I didn't. I thought I had the solution when I remembered our travelling fish salesman. I knew he had told me that cats streamed across the fields whenever he stopped at a farm, however isolated it might me; and that he knew by sight every cat on his rounds.

He had never before seen our little black cat. Nor had anyone told him that they had lost one. Nor were our own enquiries any more fruitful. It was a magic cat which had come out of the moorland and the cliffs to prove to me that impossible conditions could be fulfilled. I had to admit defeat. The cat could stay; and she enriched our lives ever after.

We called her Lama because the Dalai Lama had escaped from Tibet at the time; and it seemed they had something in common in the sense they had both escaped from danger. A silly comparison, of course, but animals usually receive their names for silly reasons. And we had given her the name before we realised her sex. I thought she was a boy . . . until on the second night Sammy, an active tom from the farm at the top of the lane, jumped through our bedroom window and on to the bed where Lama was sleeping in Jeannie's arms. 'Lama's a girl,' I shouted hysterically from my pillow, imagining litters of kittens, 'we must get her to the vet straightaway tomorrow!'

Since that day she went to the vet, she never went further than a half mile from Minack. The vet said she was about five months old and, as no one could trace where she had come from, it was reasonable to guess that she had been born out in the wild; and she had been foraging on her own for many weeks. I later had one report of her during this time from Joe Richards who looked after the cliff meadows of my neighbour. Joe told me he had seen a little black cat in the old quarry, the quarry which long ago was used to provide stone for the local lanes. He had seen it there a few times, but never further west. Joe was one of those country-men who might notice a mouse moving in a meadow.

He and I and Jeannie once succeeded in saving the life of a badger which Joe himself had caught in a gin trap (in the days when gin traps were legal). Joe hated gin traps in any case, but the farmer had asked him to catch rabbits; and gin traps were the means to catch them, and occasionally a badger or a fox would be caught in their place. On this occasion Joe found a handsome badger in one of the traps and, knowing that he would not be able to release it unless he knocked it unconscious, he brought his stick down with a bang on its head. The badger was knocked out, and then Joe began to worry. Had he knocked him too hard? He there-upon released him from the trap, collected his heavy body in his arms, and carried it down to the Pink Hut near the quarry.

The Pink Hut is still there. We used to have half of it, Joe the other half, and here we used to 'shoot' the potato seed we needed . . . for we rented many of the surrounding meadows. They were not healthy meadows because they had become tired from years and years of potato growing; and to put them in good heart again they required much farmyard manure which we couldn't obtain. Joe's meadows below the Pink Hut were, however, the best potato meadows in the district; and the earliest for that matter. Our potatoes were still the size of white marbles at the time he had begun to dig his meadows for market; and we would watch him shovelling away, filling the chip baskets, with envy. It was a pastoral scene. Fishing boats of Newlyn and Mousehole below us chugging to and from the fishing grounds around Land's End. Gannets diving off shore, swallows skimming the rocks, the scrape of the shovel in soil, the sense of the world standing still. Nothing, it seemed, to stop this mood from continuing for ever and ever; and then one day we saw a wooden stake driven into the ground near the quarry where Joe had seen Lama. Always beware of wooden stakes.

They are the harbingers of development, of material progress; and this wooden stake was the first sign that a lighthouse was to be built below the Pink Hut and the quarry. Not long after there were further developments. We had now given up renting the surrounding meadows, and Joe also had gone, and the farm had changed hands. The new owner listened to the professors of progress, and obeyed them . . . bulldozing the ancient hedges of his farm to create prairie size fields, heaping the old stones in huge lorries and dumping the debris above the old quarry; and among that debris was the multitude of small creatures which inhabited the hedges. This pyre was added to by empty polythene fertiliser bags, blue and white, broken broccoli boxes, odd bits of iron. There are other changes too. The tall privet hedges which surrounded the meadows we worked have been cut down. These acts have been done in the cause of increased production. Nobody can be blamed. For we live in a functional age. Believers in beauty should not interfere.

But the morning Joe carried the badger to the Pink Hut, we were still living life slowly. Joe could perform such a gesture without being self conscious about it. No one would accuse him of wasting his time. No one would ask him why he was doing it. No one would try to reason with him that there were more important tasks in his day than saving the life of a badger. He was fulfilling a pattern of the countryside that was personally more rewarding than any pay award. And I remember his pleasure when some weeks later, Jeannie and I having shared the task of nursing the badger, the three of us arrived at the Pink Hut one morning . . . and found the floor boards ripped apart. The badger was well enough to join his world again.

Lama, on the other hand, never wanted to be part of the wild again. She clung to us. I would see her stroll down the lane to Monty's Leap, sip from the little stream, and sometimes wander through the gap into the field where stood the mobile greenhouses. She would stalk mice in the stable field which is below the cottage, or in the field above the cottage. But she never went far from the cottage and we never saw her on any territory except Minack territory. She had found a home, and she was not going to risk finding the home a mirage.

She had a companion in those early years . . . Boris, a Muscovy drake that Jane had brought to us. He and Lama had a respect for each other, even an affection, but they were always trying to score a point over one another. Thus Boris, if Lama was blissfully asleep in some sunny corner, would slowly plod towards her, weaving his head, until suddenly he reached her, then hissed; and Lama would leap away in fright. Lama would, in due course, try to win her revenge. Her efforts, I fear, were never very successful. She would be lying in wait beside the cottage door for Boris's regular evening arrival, an arrival which was rewarded with the titbits which Jeannie had ready for him. Then, from her waiting place, Lama would appear, expecting that her fierce face and the spitting noise she uttered would put Boris to flight. But Boris was far too sure of himself for that to happen. He just looked at Lama, extended his neck to and fro, hissed a little; and then set upon the titbits.

Meanwhile we continued to wonder where she had come from, and it was like following the tantalising clues of a treasure hunt. We soon realised that no human was ever going to help us. Our enquiries about her had now ranged so widely that the possibility of her coming from any village or farm within reasonable distance was out of the question. Any clue about her, therefore, had to be found nearer home, and we found this clue in a most unexpected way.

Some while before Lama came on to the scene, a small grey cat had haunted the area. We had often noticed her as she meandered across our meadows, or hunted for mice, or sat on a rock sunning herself, for she had a neat little body and a pretty head; and later, on Lama's arrival, Jeannie said one day how very alike in size and shape they both were.

But this grey cat made it quite plain that she wanted nothing to do with us. She scorned Jeannie's blandishments, and I watched amusedly Jeannie's failure. Jeannie was not accustomed to be rebuffed by cats, even a wild one like this grey one. Yet in the years ahead it was to be proved that she had in some way established an understanding . . . Daisy, as we had come to call the wanderer, found her way to Minack when she was dying; and in the last few days of her life, though still refusing to sacrifice her independence, let Jeannie try to help her. She hung around by Monty's Leap, sheltering among the heliotrope leaves that border the bank, refusing the food Jeannie offered her, but in the end allowing Jeannie to pick her up and carry her into the greenhouse; the only time Jeannie ever touched her. That day I gave her a saucer of water and Daisy, as if to show how angry she was with herself for asking help from a human, violently brought a paw down on the saucer; and broke it. An hour later she had died.

The clue, however, she gave us happened three years before. Geoffrey was planting bulbs with another man, a casual help, one early September afternoon, in one of the lower meadows of the cliff. There they were digging at the soil when Geoffrey paused for a moment because he thought he saw a movement among some brush at the top of the meadow. That is one of the pleasures of working amongst nature. An odd sound, an odd movement, and the senses are alert. In this case Geoffrey was astonished to find that the odd movement was that of a small black kitten. It was on its own, playing among the roots of brambles, oblivious of what was happening several yards away from it. Oblivious only for a second; and when Geoffrey began walking towards it, it speedily disappeared into the undergrowth. Of course, as soon as he came back to the cottage, he told Jeannie; and her reaction was predictable. She was writing her novel *Hotel Regina* at the time, forcing herself to keep steady hours. Such good intentions, however, could justifiably be forgotten by news such as Geoffrey brought. A black kitten down the cliff? This was a matter which had immediately to be investigated. It was an extraordinary situation; and so she left her typewriter, and ran away down to the meadow where Geoffrey had last seen it. Not a sign. She looked in one meadow, then another; and she was only aware of a robin watching her, and a stonechat on a bramble tendril jerking its head. Then, just as she was about to return disappointed, she had a look into the miniature cave half-way down the cliff. There, curled on a bed of dried grass was the black kitten.

It was Daisy's kitten, of course. We saw her down the cliff that evening from where we were hiding behind the branches of the elderberry hedge. Jeannie had quietly taken a saucer of bread and milk to the entrance of the miniature cave; and we were waiting for the kitten to come out and eat it. Daisy passed it, didn't hesitate and dashed into the miniature cave. For six days Jeannie filled the saucer with fresh bread and milk, but only on the first three days was it eaten. Thereupon a neurosis developed. Perhaps the bread and milk had been bait for a fox; and the fox had found the hideout of the kitten, and eaten it as well as the bread and milk. We became increasingly anxious. Both Daisy and the kitten had vanished yet leaving us with a maddening suspicion. Daisy was the shape and size of Lama, and the black kitten, as Jeannie said, was also exactly like Lama; and the maddening suspicion was that we might have at last discovered Lama's secret . . . Daisy was Lama's mother, and Lama too was born in the miniature cave. We were never to know for certain, there would never be enough evidence to satisfy a jury. But Jeannie has no doubts that the suspicion was justified. She has a fey mind, and does not need logic to prove what she believes.

Meanwhile what had happened to them? I consoled Jeannie with her fears about the fox by saying that we were probably the cause of their disappearance. We had shown too much interest. We had scared Daisy into taking the kitten away to another hideout, some other part of the cliff we could not reach; and that we had ourselves to blame for behaving like interfering do-gooders. Daisy's independence was more important to her than a saucer of bread and milk for her kitten.

But on the Friday afternoon, a week after Geoffrey first saw the kitten, we saw Daisy again; and then a second time,

22

in more strange circumstances, as dusk was falling.

We were about to lock up Boris in his house in the wood, and at the same time we were calling for Lama. We hadn't seen her for a while, and we wanted her indoors for her evening meal. Suddenly Jeannie called out: 'Look up there in that elm tree!' On one of the branches several feet from the ground were two shapes close to each other. One shape was that of Lama, the other that of Daisy. There was no sense of tension between them. They were obviously friendly; and the sight was the more astonishing because in all the years Daisy had been around, I had never before seen her remain for any length of time so close to the cottage.

'They look like plotters,' said Jeannie jokingly. Then added: 'But what has she done with the kitten?'

The following morning soon after breakfast, Jeannie asked me to fetch an onion from the string of them we kept hung over a beam in the barn. It was a very old barn with a cobbled floor, and feet thick walls built with slabs of granite bound together by clay. The battered stable door faced towards the sea. The opposite wall lined the lane, and cut into the wall were two small windows; and these two windows were to be much looked through during the course of the next few days. For when I arrived at the stable door which had been left open, I found in front of me curled on a sack in the centre of the barn, the black kitten.

The discovery naturally caused great excitement; and Jeannie promptly set in motion all the usual cat lover fuss. Once again, however, she was frustrated. The kitten wanted nothing to do with her. As soon as she arrived with a saucer of milk, the kitten dashed behind a mountain of boxes and lumber we kept in a corner of the barn. She was also frustrated by the bewildering way the kitten had appeared in the barn. Daisy must have led it there. But why? Did she expect Lama to accept it as a companion? Lama, however, during the course of the next few days, displayed no interest in the barn whatsoever.

We did. Jeannie would go to the barn with her saucer, then run round the lane, and peer through one of the windows. In due course the kitten would timidly come away from its hiding place, and advance towards the saucer. We now could examine it carefully; and it was extraordinary how exactly it resembled a very young Lama. It was totally black. It had the same shaped head, and the same texture of coat. Only the tail was different; it was thin compared to Lama's. But I could understand why Jeannie was certain they shared the same mother.

So we watched, myself in a detached way, Jeannie in the hope that the kitten would one day show its appreciation of her efforts. We watched, for instance, the peculiar way it drank the milk from the saucer. The usual cat drinks neatly. The kitten, however, buried its face into the milk so that when the saucer was dry, its face looked as if it had been dipped into snow. We were amused, but saw no significance in its behaviour.

The kitten stayed in the barn for ten days; and then one morning I said to Jeannie, after the saucer of milk had been left untouched, that I was sure the barn was empty and that I felt we would never see the kitten again.

Perhaps we never did. Perhaps the kitten died, or wandered miles and miles away. I will never be sure. All I can tell you is that a black cat with a thin tail, and the unusual habit of burying its face into a saucer of milk *did* one day come to Minack.

THREE

Jeannie had given the name of Rosebud to the kitten; and so during its brief stay in the barn there were frequent remarks such as : 'I'm taking the saucer down to Rosebud.' Or : 'Let's look through the barn window and watch Rosebud.' And then later, after the kitten had disappeared, there were such musings as : 'I wonder what happened to Rosebud?' or : 'Do you think a fox caught Rosebud?' Rosebud, therefore, had become a ghost personality in our household.

Jeannie's interest was, of course, greater than mine. Cat lovers' vanity is easily wounded, and I am sure she was irked by the manner in which Rosebud had ignored her. One evening, during the stay in the barn, Rosebud had, however, touched her. It was at night when Jeannie had gone down to the barn; and she had almost reached it when she was aware that something was, for a brief moment, brushing her leg; and then a second later she saw a black shadow dash away from her. This was the first physical contact with the kitten who had the habit of burying its face in a saucer of milk; and Jeannie was never to forget it. She was tantalised by this contact, and by the background of the story; and by the mystery of Rosebud's disappearance. And from that moment she was always looking for Rosebud.

I was too.

One of the charms of living in the country is the possession of time in which to delve into trivial mysteries. It was always so. I imagine the questions of those who have lived in Minack cottage . . . what is that strange ship sailing past Carn Barges towards Newlyn, and where has she come from? Why have the badgers abandoned the sett down the cliff this spring? Who is that walking through the bracken on the other side of the valley? Did you hear the chiff chaff this morning, first one of the year? What killed the moorhen, was it a hawk? Why was a dog fox calling outside the cottage for the second night running? Why do gulls float from the west at night to rest on the rocks facing east?

I can imagine these people who lived their lives at Minack puzzling over these minor problems. Such events served no purpose except momentarily to occupy their attention. A diversion to their day which possessed no significance. They were pursuing the languid journey from birth to marriage to death, uncluttered by the side issues which fill, or empty, the society of today. They were enjoying, and quite unselfconscious that they were doing so, a natural life.

These ghosts of Minack have left their impression. I sense their presence. How, I sometimes wonder, would they face the problems which Jeannie and I face today? For, although we may still possess the kind of freedom which is denied those who are forced by circumstances to lead routine lives, we are aware that the theorists are catching up on us. We have become, like everyone else, units in the national computer, and we are now the servants of Mr Average; and we no longer can sentimentally pretend we are isolated from the herd. We gaze wondrously at statistical reports and discover what we do. We play Bingo twice a week, place Crossroads at the top of the charts, eat more bananas than we did two years ago, go less often to football matches, drink more beer, and are unfulfilled because we have no telephone in the house.

Such examples of Mr Average may seem trivial, but there is an underlying significance about them which is disquieting. For the cult of Mr Average fools people into believing that we are all equal; and we are not, whatever the politicians and union leaders may say. The bleat of fair shares for all is as futile as the expectation that all horses, hacks, hunters and selling platers have an equal chance of winning the Derby. We can't all be a Gauguin or a Churchill or a Mozart or a Nicklaus or a Jane Austen or a Margot Fonteyn.

Yet the mood of this age urges us to be indignant if we are not, or to be full of self-pity; and the result is a barren philosophy of envy which leads people to believe that rewards come as a right, and not as a consequence of talent, luck, and endeavour. The cult of Mr Average taunts us to disregard ourselves as individuals. Our contrariness, our complexity, our special likes and dislikes, our subtle emotions which often surprise ourselves, are ignored when the computer does its work. It only seeks one result . . . the materialistic Mr Average.

One observes Mr Average in detachment until one becomes involved with him. Jeannie and I suddenly became aware of our involvement when it was decreed that the wage of the agricultural worker, being below the national average, was to be increased by £3.55 a week resulting in a £7 a week increase within a year; and with the promise of similar annual increases in the future.

Such a wage award programme is admirable in theory. It assumes that any business, whatever its nature or financial situation, is morally bound to pay out wages it cannot afford; or, alternatively, it assumes that pound notes flutter from the sky into the lap of an employer whenever a wage award is granted. Many concerns, of course, counter by higher prices, higher fares, higher rates, and higher charges for other affected services . . . with consequent squeals from the very same people who pressed for the higher wages. But there is a host of small businesses that cannot cope with this sudden leap in annual wage rises of pounds instead of shillings; and their end is in sight.

It is sad because small businesses can often offer job satisfaction which is impossible in large concerns; and job satisfaction, although a dirty phrase in the minds of some, as if it reflects a pleasure which has been deceitfully invented by an employer to dupe his staff, offers a base for a happy life. Those, for instance, who work on the land have this job satisfaction. The sky is their factory ceiling, they do not have the expense and weariness of travelling to work on crowded trains and roads, they breathe unpolluted air, and they have nature around them to provide them with diversions.

It is lucky for us that Geoffrey appreciates these things, and there is never a day when one of us does not comment to the other about some aspect of the country scene. But we still have to be realistic, and try to make the market garden pay . . . and market gardeners, unlike farmers, have no Price Review which helps to compensate farmers with guaranteed prices to cover their increased costs. Market gardeners, instead, are dependent on the open market, and the weather; and, although prices for their produce may have risen substantially in the shops, their own returns have actually declined, not risen, in recent years.

Nor can market gardeners mechanise their methods of work with the comparative ease that farmers can. There is no machine to pick an acre of daffodils, then bunch and pack them; or a machine which is capable of pinching out unnecessary growth in tomato plants, or picking the fruit when they ripen. Hence market gardeners have no alternative to hand labour; and hand labour is pricing itself away from reality.

It was a year after Rosebud had disappeared from the barn that we had our first false alarm. I looked out of the bathroom window into the field we call the donkey field, an acre of green grass where the donkeys spend much of their time; and saw the little black head of Lama peering from a thicket of coarse grass which the donkeys, for pernickety reasons, had decided not to eat.

'Lama,' I called to Jeannie, 'is in the donkey field hunting rabbits.'

'She isn't,' I heard her call back, 'she's on my lap, and she's stopping me from putting the bread in the oven.'

Cats, as many people know, stop you from *doing* things. I think, perhaps, that this is one of the reasons why I tried for so long not to become a cat lover. I feared cats. Dogs were wonderfully comforting because they *wanted* to love and be loved. Cats were aloof things. They judged humanity in a cool, remote fashion which was unnerving to anyone who was a dog lover. A dog increases a man's confidence, a cat can dim it; and I have known dog lovers to be so unnerved by the presence of a cat that they have set a trap for it; and then removed it from the neighbourhood. All this I can understand since I was born to be anti-cat, and remained anti-cat for so many years of my life.

'How extraordinary,' I called back again, 'the cat I am looking at must be the double of Lama.'

'A moment and I'll be with you.'

I could see in my mind how 'the moment' would be spent . . . the careful transfer of Lama from lap to sofa, and the murmur of sweet nothings as she did so. Jeannie might be inquisitive about Rosebud, but Lama would always be her Queen.

But as I said, it was a false alarm. Just as Jeannie reached me the cat moved away from its grassy hideout, and though the body was black it had a dirty white leg. It was also a large cat.

'Too large for Rosebud in any case.'

'And Rosebud didn't have a spot of white.'

I watched the cat move away down the field, then over the hedge alongside the wood. I had never seen the cat before, and I didn't expect to see him again, nor did I want to do so. I was, for Lama's sake, apprehensive about large tom cats. I remembered a warning given me that farm tom cats were notorious for the way they hunted neutered females, and killed them if given the chance. The warning was given me when Lama first came to Minack by a lady who was as amused at my worried reaction as she was interested in safeguarding Lama's future.

'It isn't one of Walter's cats,' said Jeannie, 'I'm sure of that.'

There is a higgledy piggledy collection of farm buildings at the top of our lane on the way to the main road; and two small farmhouses. In one of them live our friends the Trevorrows, and the name of Trevorrow is one of the oldest in Cornwall. For many years Mrs Trevorrow has taken in visitors during the summer, and she is famous for her good food; and when we have a girl from afar to work for us during the flower season, Mrs Trevorrow gives a temporary home to the girl. A hundred yards away is the farmhouse of the Cockram family. Jack Cockram was an evacuee from London during the war and learned his skills as a farm worker at a farm not far away; and then one day I was able to help him become a tenant farmer, and his farm now spreads out from the higgledy piggledy farm buildings, the haphazardly placed fields, mingling with those of the Trevorrows. Both these families have been wonderful friends to us. I remember asking Bill Trevorrow very early on when we came to Minack, if he could help us out by ploughing a steep piece of ground in which we wanted to plant potatoes. Next morning he was there; and I took a photograph of him as he sat poised on his tractor before beginning his task. I remember at that moment thinking how wrong it was of me to ask him as a favour to take on something so seemingly dangerous. Yet he knew what he was doing. He would not have offered to do it unless he had the measure of it. In the many years I have known Bill Trevorrow, I have learnt that that is the criterion by which he is guided.

Walter Grose is the third farmer at the top of the lane, and for many years he was tenant of yet a third farm which spread out from the higgledy piggledy buildings, but after Jack Cockram came along they joined up together in partnership. Walter, a bachelor, however, did not live at the farm, his house was in St Buryan village, and he used to travel to work by van early every morning and return late at night. A long day among the fields and his cows . . . and his cats.

He had numerous cats which lived around the farm buildings, black and white cats, cats with brown smudged faces and brown and white bodies, patchy grey cats; and, of course, numerous kittens, half grown cats and somnolent elderly cats. They waited expectantly for his arrival in the morning, then gathered around the van as he produced their breakfast; and they gathered around the van again when he had his crust when he had his dinner, when he had his tea. Walter was a Pied Piper of cats.

Of course so many cats could cause problems. Mrs Trevorrow, for instance, though devoted to all animals including cats, was naturally perturbed when a Walter cat appeared on her kitchen window sill. Jack Cockram, I suspect, also viewed the cats with apprehension. But what could anyone do? Walter would sit in his van having his tea out of a thermos, or munching sandwiches, and there were his cats . . . on the bonnet, around the wheels, comfortable and purring, aware that here was a man who would look after them, feeding them with a continual supply of fashionable tins of cat food.

Naturally other farm cats were attracted to the scene. Eager tom cats stepped across the fields; and from time to time the great barn which housed the hay became a maternity home for kittens; and corners of it would nurture small families of Walter fed cats.

I came up the lane one April morning at the time of our first Rosebud alarm, and saw Walter bending down, fingering the leaf of Hart's Tongue fern which was growing in the bank. This fern is named after the tongue of a fully grown deer, and it is pale green, delicate in texture, with slender tongue shaped leaves.

'Lovely,' he said, without looking up, 'man couldn't make anything as lovely as this.'

'They pay to have it in their gardens up country,' I said practically, 'and yet we can see it growing naturally, taking it almost for granted.'

'Never,' said Walter, 'never can take nature for granted.'

An old countryman, like Walter, is caught between his proved contentment in the way of life of his past and the necessity of being on the bandwagon of twentieth century progress. Any countryman, for that matter, is in the same trap. He distrusts city type standards, yet seems to have little power to resist them. The cement based apostles of progress have a charisma which the countryman cannot match. The countryman, rich in the minor matters of life, has no persuasive answer to those who demand more land, more land, and still more land for housing estates, motorways, schools and factories. The countryman watches the badger setts, home for a thousand years of badgers, demolished within the hour by a monster machine; or that of a fox's earth, or the site of a long used heron's nest, or hedges and undergrowth where warblers, chiff chaffs, whitethroats make their nests after flying thousands of miles to do so. But what arguments can he produce to prove that the preservation of such minor matters is more important than yielding to the materialism of the human race?

'When I was young,' said Walter, 'we went looking for plants like these, and wild flowers, and there was excitement in finding them. It wasn't just the few who did this, most of us felt the same way.'

'You didn't have the advantages, Walter, of television and cars and motorcycles.'

'What advantages? Are they happier racing back to watch a programme than I was finding a patch of wild violets mixed with primroses?'

'Up in the village yesterday,' I said, 'I saw a group outside the church gates listening to a transistor placed on the roof of a car. They seemed happy enough.'

Perhaps there were half a dozen in the group and the neighbourhood was suffering. It was a terrible noise.

'But we youngsters kept to ourselves,' said Walter, 'we would never think of upsetting other people. We would have been in trouble if we did. There was discipline in those days.'

There are those who shut their minds to the past, as if it had nothing to teach them. They brag about never looking back, a boast which seems to me to deny them the advantage of learning from their mistakes. They pursue their lives as if each day was an entity instead of part of the whole, and they explain their attitude by proclaiming they are modern. The moderns, they say, only look to the future.

'I enjoyed Sunday School,' Walter went on, 'and I didn't mind the three mile walk each way because we made it an adventure. We used to look out for the wild flowers and grasses, and make them into posies and take them home as presents . . . past where the airport is now, fields in those days, and along the lane down to the chapel in Nanquidno.'

The airport today is a curse to all those who live near it, and especially to those who live in the straddling village of Sennen Cove, and in Cot Valley. Instead of looking out onto the Atlantic and listening to the sound of the surf rolling up onto the long stretch of sands and rocks, the inhabitants have to endure the rasping engines of small aircraft droning overhead. The airport is the base of a flying club which may give pleasure to a few but, like the group who hung around the transistor outside St Buryan church, ruin the peace of everyone else.

'Then there were the harvest festivals . . . they really were harvest festivals in those days. We brought our offerings for the decoration of the chapel because we truly believed we were giving thanks for the harvest. It was not done for effect. The whole year revolved around the gathering of the harvest, and because there weren't the machines of these days, we felt so much more grateful for what nature had given us. We were so much closer to nature then. It was both our master and our friend.'

'What happened?' I asked, and it was mischievous of me to ask, 'if the harvest had been a bad one?'

Walter took me seriously.

'That made no difference,' he said, 'we brought our gifts in thankfulness for living.'

'You were lucky, Walter, to have such a simple philosophy. Most people would laugh at it now.'

'Everyone's too clever.'

'And living too fast.'

Walter can only see through one eye. The other was blinded by a flying stone when he was helping to repair the farm lane many years ago, before we came to Minack. It

3   33

worries him, of course, but I have seldom heard him mention it.

'Funny thing,' he said, 'I remember when it all changed.'

'How do you mean?'

'Milk,' he went on, 'never used to be collected on Sundays, the Sabbath being what it was.'

'But the cows had to be milked, didn't they?'

'Ah yes, but that was the only work that was done, no kind of business was ever conducted.'

Thus the churns of Saturday evening milking, and of Sunday morning and Sunday evening, were kept back for the Monday collection.

'Then one day grandfather heard a rumour there might be Sunday collection before long, and I remember him solemnly saying to me: "The day they change to collecting milk on a Sunday ... all else will follow." '

Walter hadn't changed much at any rate. He still worked seventy and more hours a week, always had a pleasant word for any passer-by, still replied to the question, 'How are you, Walter?' with the answer, 'Poor but happy', and still had his cats.

The black cat with the dirty white leg didn't belong to him as Jeannie had said. We never knew where it came from. It would roam around Minack for a day or two, then disappear for weeks; and when it returned, when one morning I would see its face peering among the grass in the donkey field above the cottage, I would call out to Jeannie that the tom cat was back. And immediately I would be on guard about Lama.

The second false alarm had more substance. Carol, a girl secretary from Nottingham had called on us, and wanted to look at the cottage where Jane of *A Drake at the Door* had lived. The cottage was empty at the time (it has now been rebuilt along with the two cottages on either side and made into one house), and I gave the girl directions how to get there, ten minutes away, through the Pentewan meadows.

An hour later the girl returned from her pilgrimage, and surprised us by saying she had met a black cat by the old quarry. Jeannie and I reacted to the news in predictable ways. I ignored it, Jeannie insisted she had to make an investigation; and she went off the same evening to look for it.

She found nothing. The next day we walked over to the quarry together, then the following day, and the day after that. Not a sign of a cat. 'The girl imagined it,' I said to Jeannie.

But Jeannie was persistent. There was a full moon the following night, and once again she set off for the quarry, alone this time, leaving me to wallow in a bath. Then twenty minutes later I heard her call excitedly, and I clambered out, wrapping myself in a towel, and found Jeannie in the sitting room holding a saucer in either hand.

'I've found it,' she cried, as if she had found a mislaid valuable brooch, 'and it's outside there in the garden!'

I looked round for Lama and saw her in a deep sleep on the sofa. She was unaware of the unfaithfulness.

'What happened?'

'It just appeared out of one of the meadows, and came up to me, and when I turned to come back it followed. It's a he, that I'm sure, and I call him Felix.'

Still wrapped in my bath towel, I stepped outside and peered at Felix who now was devouring a saucer of fish which Lama would have had for breakfast in the morning.

'That certainly is not Rosebud,' I said immediately, and rather crossly, 'and he certainly isn't one of Daisy's offspring.' Daisy, the neat, small grey wild cat, mother of Lama and Rosebud. 'He's leggy, and bony,' I went on, 'and he has a small head, and he's very skinny . . .'

'He's starving!'

'Don't fool yourself that this is Rosebud returned. This is just a black cat which has been abandoned . . . and he's looking for a new home. We'll have trouble unless you get rid of him quickly.'

'How quickly?'

'Tonight!'

This was, of course, bravado talk on my part. It was too late to do anything. All we could do was to shut the door on

35

him, and pray he would be gone in the morning. He wasn't. He had made himself a nest in the tractor shelter, enjoyed an excellent sleep after his first decent meal in weeks . . . and now was ready for more. There he was, looking through the sitting room window, confidently staring at me, while Lama was at my feet rubbing against my leg.

'Jeannie,' I said authoritatively, 'we couldn't get rid of him last night BUT this morning . . .'

There are people I know who have thick skins. They simply refuse to accept the fact they are not wanted, and they will mooch around, or bossily try to take charge, without taking note of any hint that they should buzz off.

Felix was one of these. During the course of the following five days, he resolutely refused to take note of my obvious distaste for his presence. He had found a home, and nothing was going to budge him from it . . . and budge him we certainly tried.

Our first step was to discover that he belonged to a recently sold farm which was now empty. Adjacent to this farm was another farm, and its owner was a good friend of mine, and a lover of cats. Both farms were a mile or so from Minack as the crow flies, across a number of fields, and out of sight. We called on my friend, and he happily agreed that he would look after Felix if we brought him back.

This we did. We picked Felix up, sat him on Jeannie's lap in the car while I drove, and took him round to his benefactor. That was Monday afternoon. By Tuesday midday he was back at Minack, his radar system guiding him across the fields. Once again we picked him up, put him in the car, and took him to my friend. Wednesday afternoon he was back again. Once more we returned him. Thursday there was no sign of him, and I felt relaxed. Friday he suddenly appeared just as some visitors were taking a photograph of Lama . . . and the subsequent print included him. Felix was clinging to us, and I had become desperate.

'We must telephone his previous owner,' I said to Jeannie, 'he may be so distressed by the story that he will have Felix back.'

As we have no telephone, we suffer the minor inconvenience of driving to the telephone kiosk at Sparnon on the way to Land's End or at Sheffield near Paul, or sometimes driving into Penzance to the Queen's Hotel facing the sea on the promenade. Jeannie remembers this hotel as a child when she used to stay there with her parents on the way to the Scillies, and she remembers two members of the staff particularly. Frank in the bar who catered for her father; and Billy, the head porter, whose good nature catered for everyone. Both were still at their posts when we were attempting to solve Felix's future.

Felix's future, however, was decided upon at the Sparnon kiosk. On the Friday, I sat outside the Sparnon kiosk with skinny Felix on my lap while Jeannie talked to the previous owner; and I watched her through the glass gesticulating with one hand, and I guessed she was getting nowhere in her plea that he should take possession again of his abandoned Felix. Jeannie can be persuasive, and determined, but she was bluntly told that the man's new home was too small for a cat, and that she could do what she liked with him.

But just after she had given me her account of the conversation, I suddenly saw coming along the road towards us a tractor and trailer, and driving the tractor was the young man who had become the new owner of the farm. This was a blessed moment of good fortune, and I seized it. I jumped out of the car, ran across the road and stopped him.

'I need your help!' I cried.

The young man was not going to live at his new farm, for he already had another. His plan was to cultivate the fields, and sell off the farmhouse as a private residence. He had already, thanks to an introduction I had given him, sold the three cottages in one of which Jane had once lived; and, therefore, he was in a way in my debt. He could pay his debt by accepting Felix.

He needed no persuasion.

'O.K.,' he said, looking down on me from the tractor, 'as I bought the farm I reckon I am responsible for what went

37

with it . . . we have enough cats as it is, mind, but I guess the children will be glad to have another.'

So ended the Felix saga. The second, and last, of the Rosebud false alarms.

FOUR

Lama was with me while I wrote my books about Minack. She planted her muddy paws on the first page of the manuscript of this book; and I treated it as lucky that she had done so. Even in my anti-cat days, as I have said, a black cat was an emblem of good luck. I was never superior about this superstition; and I always felt happier if a black cat crossed my path. A nanny may have planted the idea in the first place, or perhaps it was my mother. My mother disliked cats, but she had an intuitive mind, a mind which could dispense with hard reason. All through my growing up she shared my hopes, talking on my behalf in family councils, giving me confidence in practical ways; and displaying more than once the queer power of the spirit which has influenced me ever since.

My father, when he was a child, had a nurse called Miss Lewin; and after Miss Lewin had completed her life of looking after other people's children, she retired to Ilfracombe. For what seemed to be to me many young years of my own life, we were always about to visit Miss Lewin, but for one reason or another there was always some good cause for the visit to be postponed.

Then at last the great day arrived. Today we *will* visit Miss Lewin; and it was my mother who decided this, for my father at the time was away. Perhaps my mother, in her wish to provide a diversion for a school holiday, believed it would provide me, and my two brothers, with an adventure. Unfortunately she had lost Miss Lewin's address.

It is vague now in my mind as to how we reached Ilfracombe, except I seem to remember my mother at the wheel of our four-seater Morris open tourer, repeatedly blowing the horn at cattle blocking the way as we careered up the north coast of Cornwall into Devon. My mother was an excellent driver, and she was one of the first women ever to drive a car from London to Cornwall . . . although at the time she was incapable of reversing. On one pioneer journey to Cornwall she accompanied my father; and as they droned their way further and further west, the car became slower and slower. At last they reached Lanivet, the village outside Bodmin on the way to Goss Moor, and began to climb up the hill on the other side. The car had lost its energy. The engine stuttered, the whole machine behaved like a long distance runner who had gone beyond his limit, puff-puff, would it ever reach the top? Then, just before it reached the top, the car and its occupants, suffered a monstrous indignity. A donkey pulling a cart caught up with them . . . and passed.

We reached Ilfracombe, and I was impressed by the Victorian heaviness of the place. Solid houses with porticos, solid streets, solid shops, solid people in the streets. But where was Miss Lewin?

There then occurred the event which impressed me for ever afterwards . . . we had wandered around for an hour or more when suddenly my mother pointed to a solid house in the centre of the town, one in a long avenue, and declared: 'If we knock at that door I'm sure we'll find her.'

We did. Miss Lewin was in the sitting room, ninety years old and blind, but I had been so amazed by my mother's intuition that I remember nothing of the old nurse herself.

The incident left a profound impression upon me because it was the first time I became aware that intuition was stronger than logic. We may draw up sensible plans, proliferate our lives with rules and regulations, have years of study and training, and yet it is intuition which keeps the key. A doctor's diagnosis, the swerving run of a three-quarter, the success of a political leader, the achievements of a business man, the skill of a teacher, all in the final instance depend on intuition.

I consoled myself with these thoughts when I was young, because I was never conventionally successful at school. The tangible establishment successes eluded me. My eldest brother Colin, for instance, was captain of the Haileybury rugby team, and head of his house; and my other elder brother Nigel won the award of the King's Dirk at Dartmouth, the Royal Navy equivalent of the Sword of Honour at Sandhurst. But I, at Harrow, achieved no honour at all. 'Useless to society,' was the comment about me by my housemaster on one occasion after I had missed a catch in the outfield during an inter-house match.

I was useless, too, academically. I failed examination after examination, and as school leaving time approached this naturally caused anxiety to my parents and others in the family circle. What future has he? What job can we find him? As for myself I was not all that concerned by my failures. I disturbed my schoolmasters, and thus I was not in fear of their opinions of me. I believed, as schoolboys have believed in other generations, that I was only of interest to them as examination fodder. My own ideas of education were very different, though unfortunately impractical. I wanted to be prepared for the world which was waiting for me, and when one day I read Ernest Raymond's *Through Literature to Life*, a book which dazzled me with its enlightenment, I drew up a schedule of my ideal form of education. I would leave Harrow when I was sixteen, spend one year studying English literature, a second year French literature, a third year learning to play the piano, a fourth year studying European art, and a fifth year becoming knowledgeable about wine and fine food. At twenty-one, therefore, I would be equipped, so I believed, to enjoy my life.

Instead, I continued to stalk Harrow hill; and by the time I reached the conventional age of leaving, I had come to realise that I did not belong to the society in which I had spent the previous five years. I was a loner. I could never belong to the club. I would never flourish if I sought to follow the tribal customs of the establishment. There were edges about me that would never fit. I hated groups. I considered groups as a collection of people who were running away from their secret selves, deliberately drowning reality by herd thinking. I would never be recognised as 'one of them'. I was awkward, and unpredictable; and unpredictability is the worst sin you can commit in the judgement of the establishment.

All through this period, and after, my mother sustained me. She had no ambitions for her sons except that we should be happy, and my own attitudes, however different they may have been from my brothers', did not deter her for an instant from helping me. Her intuition was at work again. She sensed that what I was seeking was worthwhile however nebulous it might appear to others, and to myself for that matter. Thus, when after three years as a clerk in Unilever I visited a phrenologist in Ludgate Circus who informed me that I should be an interior decorator or a journalist, she delightfully joined my enthusiasm that I should leave Unilever. For four months she and my father thereupon financed me, an out of work clerk, a hopeful would-be journalist, living in a sitting room in Jubilee Place off the Kings Road. Then luck, the most essential ingredient of anyone's life, gave me an introduction to Max Aitken; and a month later I was on trial on the northern *Daily Express* in Manchester.

I would never have been there, unless it had been for my mother's unsupported faith in me. No logic, you see, backed her. And had I been told to fill in one of those long questionnaires about myself, or attend one of those queer weekends where psychiatrists evaluate the characters of the applicants for a job by asking them futile, fancy questions, I am sure that Max Aitken (whom I have not met since that day) would never have given me the chance to go to Manchester. Both acted on intuition.

My mother presented Jeannie at Court. My mother was a fervent supporter of the Royal Family, the aristocracy and anyone else who fulfilled her definition of style. Gertrude Lawrence and Noel Coward fulfilled that definition, Claudette Colbert and Clark Gable, Cecil Beaton and A. P. Herbert, Stanley Baldwin and Helen Wills Moody. The list was select, though long because of my mother's catholic interests, and it included many figures of the past, both literary and musical. Boorishness she couldn't abide, and bad manners were unforgiveable. I am glad she didn't live to see the day of television screens being filled with placard waving louts.

My mother also had the charm of being contrary, and Jeannie's presentation at Court was a case in point.

We had no sooner been ushered through Buckingham Palace into the garden beyond when my mother disappeared. There were, of course, a large number of people attending the Garden Party, very different from my mother's presentation in King Edward Seventh's time when debutantes were ushered up to the Royal Presence one at a time. It was therefore easy to become lost in the throng unless one kept close together. One minute my mother was beside me, the next she was nowhere to be seen.

Jeannie and I were naturally distressed, and for the rest of the afternoon we walked up and down the long lawn, scanning the ladies in their finery but having no joy because we believed that my mother had lost *us*. Not at all, as it turned out. The Garden Party was at an end, the unseen instructions had been given for the guests to filter away . . . and at this moment my mother reappeared. She had had a marvellous time. She had found herself in the special enclosure reserved for the Court, the Diplomatic Corps, and members of the Government; and she had apparently quickly endeared herself to the distinguished seekers of tea, ice-cream and cakes, and with her charm and warmth this was quite understandable. She had adored it . . . and was totally unrepentant that we ourselves had wasted the great occasion frustratingly searching for her.

Lama had style. My mother never knew Lama, for she died when Monty was still alive, but I believe if she had known Lama she would have appreciated her subtle qualities just as my aunt did, my mother's sister.

My aunt, like my mother, was not cat inclined. She considered them selfish things, unbiddable, and frustrating. Her good manners were such, however, that whenever she came to Minack, and this she did once a year during the summer, she would do her best to be on friendly terms with Lama.

'Pussoo,' she would coax, 'come here, pussoo.'

Lama was never one to appreciate the kind of language many humans like to use when talking to cats. She would either ignore the speaker or look at him or her with the greatest disdain as if she were saying, 'Shut up, you idiot.' So it was poor tactics on the part of my aunt to address Lama in this way. The word 'pussoo' was enough to make Lama turn her back and stalk away.

There was another source of conflict, and this concerned the use of the spare room by my aunt, especially the use of the divan which Lama considered to be her own. Lama spent many hours of each day and night on this divan, and she saw no reason why she should not continue to do so despite the arrival of my aunt. My aunt disagreed. My aunt had always been of the firm opinion that an animal, cat or dog, had no place on a bed . . . and thus periodically during her stay I would hear, as I sat in the sitting room, harsh words coming from my aunt in the spare room. I, of course, tried to anticipate the situation by popping into the spare room every now and then, and removing Lama myself; and there was one occasion when I saved Lama from certain disaster, and my aunt from great distress. The bedclothes had been turned back, my aunt's nightdress neatly folded on the pillow . . . and Lama was curled on the nightdress.

Visit followed visit and gradually an understanding was developed between the two of them; and although my aunt was constantly thwarted when she wished to catch Lama's attention, by Lama walking off in the other direction, there were also times when Lama responded with sudden affection. An embarrassing affection on occasions. I remember, for instance, Lama coming into the cottage after she had been out in the pouring rain, then making a bee line for my aunt who was sitting on the sofa, jumping on her lap, and proceeding to lick herself dry; and my aunt didn't fancy acting as a towel. There was another occasion, a hot July afternoon, when my aunt was sitting in a deck chair in the orchard, when she was suddenly wakened from her doze by the miaows of Lama at her feet. There was also a mouse at her feet. And Lama must have wondered why my aunt, instead of displaying delight, jumped from the deck chair and hastened away.

I also have been given a mouse by Lama, and in strange circumstances. I was writing *A Drake at the Door* at the time, and one summer's day I took paper and pen down the cliff, and settled myself on the grass in one of the small meadows that lie just above the sea. It is a risky thing to do if one intends to work because, instead of working, one becomes seduced by the quiet lapping of the sea on the rocks, and slow flying gulls, and the hum of insects, and the scent of the honeysuckle which intertwines among the fuchsia, brambles and blackthorn. It is easy to doze. It is easy to forget about writing. I have often set out down the cliff with good intentions, and come back with bare pages. On this particular summer day I had been lounging in the meadow for an hour or more when to my great surprise I found Lama beside me . . . and in her mouth was a mouse which she proceeded to drop in front of me. Jeannie told me later that she had seen the mouse caught. Lama had caught three mice in quick succession near the barn, and it was the third she decided to give to me. But how did she know I was all the way down the cliff? And why did she think I would so appreciate it?

There was another incident down the cliff in which, I am sure, Lama saved me from being bitten by an adder. She has always been nonchalant in her attitude towards adders, towards anything wild for that matter. The only time I have ever known her show fear was when tom cats were on the prowl, but nothing else. I have seen her in close contact with a vixen, as if they were talking; and I have known her kill a stoat, and stink of the stoat for some time afterwards; and I have seen her play a dangerous game with an adder, boxing it with her paws as it hissed at her, though keeping her paws just out of reach of the strike.

We had had a picnic on the grass just above the grey rocks which jumble their way down to our little bay. A bottle of Côte du Rhone, home made bread, Cornish butter and Stilton . . . a banquet; and we thought of those in the Savoy Grill munching their way towards the bill. Lama was with us, and for a while she meandered down to a rock where a sliver of a stream runs, and from which she always liked to drink. Then she came back to where Jeannie and I were lying, and settled herself beside me, looking out towards the sea as we were doing.

There was a desultory, haphazard conversation.

'Funny that Lama has never been frightened by the sea.'

'She's known it since she was born.'

'How scared Monty was of it!'

'But Monty was a town cat turned countryman. Some town people never get used to the countryside because of the quiet. Monty never got used to the sea.'

Silence for a while.

'I see a big tanker on the horizon.'

Silence again.

'I never see why the visitors buy sea urchins.'

'White's had a pile in their front window yesterday.'

'They're so ugly . . . but they're good business for the skin divers.'

'The buying habits of the holidaymakers are a mystery. They buy ghastly mementoes, most of which have been made in Birmingham or Hong Kong . . . idiots. At least sea urchins are local.'

A cormorant was drying its wings on the end rock of our tiny bay, and which is known as Gazelle. A Great Black Back gull was close by, terror of the cliffs, magnificent, ready at nesting time to snatch any egg, at growing time any nestling.

'Nice seeing Mrs Reseigh yesterday.'

Her husband, Captain Reseigh, who died a few years ago,

46

was the legendary captain of the vessel which sailed between Penzance and the Scilly Isles. He never missed a trip.
However violent the storms he kept to his promise always to
maintain the link between the islands and the mainland; and
thus many flower growers owed their livelihood to him. She
had brought her grandchildren, and one was twelve-year-old
Jeremy, who had read about Lama.

'Remarkable wasn't it, the way Jeremy remembered I was
the first to touch Lama.'

More desultory conversation.

'I'll have to buy a new pair of sandals. These are worn
out.'

Suddenly Lama growled.

A cat's growl is a fearsome affair. It is so unexpected. It is
as if a dog, in a moment of great stress, miaowed. And
Lama's growl was like a rolling crescendo of bass drums.

Then I saw the adder. Black markings on its twisting grey
body, tiny head weaving . . . and barely two feet from where
I was lying.

Of course I was safe as soon as I saw it. Adders are easily
scared away, and when I brought my hand down on the
grass with a thump, and shouted, it skidded away into the
undergrowth. But it was Lama who had warned me . .
Lama's fearsome growl.

Lama, in the beginning of her life at Minack, suffered from
a disadvantage. She lived in the shadow of Monty, always
being compared to him; and there were the two pictures of
Monty which Jeannie had painted, looking down from the
walls. Monty was an imperious cat, a cat who lived through
the bombs on London, who had lived, for a cat, a glamorous
life, who used to be hailed by the crowds on Boat Race day
when he sat in the window of our home overlooking the
finishing post, wearing a light blue ribbon around his neck.
Monty, with his beautiful dark ginger stripes and white shirt
front, a haughty face, was an aristocrat of cats. And I never
expected to see any cat like him again.

Thus, although he had died, he still seemed to impose his
character on Minack when Lama came. There was the little

stream which runs across the lane at the entrance to Minack, for instance, which we call Monty's Leap. The very fact that the stream at this point was called Monty's Leap maintained his reality, a shadowy reality, of course, but a positive reminder of that evening on our first day at Minack, when he walked suspiciously down the lane, sniffing at this imaginary danger and that, then leapt across the little stream.

Hence Lama, when she came, was viewed at first only as a miraculous substitute for Monty. I was polite, but I didn't suddenly throw my love at her. Every day of the beginning I was thinking more of Monty than of Lama; and so Lama had a difficult task to perform to achieve my special affection. Jeannie, of course, was easy. Lama knew she possessed the love of Jeannie by the succulent dishes she was given, poached John Dory, chopped chicken, and creamy scrambled eggs . . . but it was equally obvious that I was remote, uninterested and unimpressed by her charms. Thus she subtly set out to change my attitude.

She would, for instance, if Jeannie and I were both sitting down, make me the choice for her flattery. She would jump on my lap, settle herself, purr compliments, and turn her head from time to time with that special cat smile which seems to say : 'I am very comfortable. I hope you are too.'

At first I responded with coolness, as if somebody had paid a call on me I had no wish to see. I would shuffle in my chair, make an exaggerated fuss as I turned the pages of my newspaper, and stare back blankly when she cast that special cat smile upon me. Then one day I placed my hand on her back, as she sat on my lap, and with a finger I traced her backbone, and without realising it I began to rub the back of her ears. There was a sudden extravaganza of purrs, waking me up to be aware of what I was doing, and to find that I was enjoying it.

Another move on her part was to follow me when I went for a stroll. I would set off along the path past the barn, pause a few minutes later to watch a bird or some other sight which had caught my attention, and discover she had come with me. Or, more effective still, I would be strolling

along and she would rush past me at great speed, then put on
the brakes when she was a few yards ahead of me, collapse
on her back, curled paws in the air, and eyes watching me to
see what I would do.

She was very pretty, very small, weighing only seven
pounds, with a black pansy of a head and a black retroussé
nose. Her eyes were unusual, the colour of almonds and
oriental to look at like those of a Burmese cat. There was
a whisper of white on the front of her, but otherwise she
was totally black except for a white whisker; and this, as she
grew older, was joined by one, two, three white whiskers,
and we would joke: 'Here comes the Chinese mandarin!'
Her coat was a special texture, silky but firm, like that of
beaver lamb.

Someone once wrote to me about her appearance after
seeing a photograph of her. And she had an odd theory to
offer. She said that Lama looked like a Polish cat, and the
reason for her theory was as follows.

She said she was living in Camborne in 1939, and once a
week two ladies in a small van from St Ives (five miles from
Minack) called at the house with home made cakes for sale.
One day one of them arrived at the door with a basket of
cakes in one hand and a basket of kittens in the other.
Among the kittens was a black one, and the Camborne lady
said she would have it. Then she was told: 'These kittens
are very different from any other around here. They are
Polish. Their parents came off a Polish ship which called at
Falmouth.' So might Lama be a descendant? Dear Lama, she
couldn't care less if she was.

Her home, after her wanderings, was miraculously real;
and her display of pleasure, her approaches to me, the
manner in which she sauntered around as if she owned
the place, her grace, and the amusement she had when the
winds blew and leaves were there for the chasing, all these
endearing qualities were soon to conquer me; and once again
I knew I had a cat who would listen to my secret thoughts.

At the time of her coming to Minack I had not tried to
write an article, certainly not a book, for nine years. I had

written, before we came here, a travel book of youthful adventure called *Time Was Mine*, and had edited a war book *Went the Day Well*, and produced a survey of the British Commonwealth with the title *One King*. I had also written a novel which I burnt. After that my mind went blank. There was no theme whatsoever which interested me; and I banished the idea of writing ever again. Words to me became meaningless. I had learnt, in any case, to be on guard against writing for the sake of writing. It is easy, in such circumstances, to find oneself writing for the entrepreneurs instead of for oneself, and financial rewards make it tempting to be corrupted. I had experienced this danger once when I was writing a column for a national daily. One day I wrote a laudatory column about a worthy charity . . . but when the editor saw my copy he ordered me to change my tone, and attack the management of the charity, a management which, from my investigations, had no cause to be attacked. I resigned that same evening from the newspaper.

But when Lama came to Minack, there had begun to be stirrings in my mind. I even placed a sheet of paper in my typewriter, and had headed it Chapter One. Weeks later the page was still blank. Months went by before the chapter was completed. Two years passed before the book was finished. And Lama herself was two.

I had ended the book with the story of Lama's arrival at Minack; and Jeannie, who drew the sketches, finished with a pert drawing of her. The consequences were very surprising to us. I had written the book, and all we now hoped for was to make some money. Then, a week after the book's publication, three ladies arrived as we were bunching daffodils in the small greenhouse.

'Can we see Lama?' one of them asked.

These three were the first of many delightful people who have been coming to Minack ever since. True I prefer to be a hermit, I feel safer if I have only myself as a companion, but I also believe that a writer, unless he is coldly professional, is lucky if he can share his story with his readers. A writer is, in any case, dependent on his readers for his livelihood; and the readers coming from all sorts of different occupations, being of all ages, and taking the trouble to find Minack when there are no directions, and it is a long way off the road, are likely to provide Jeannie and myself with a slant on life far wider than we ever knew when we lived in London. Both of us have been enriched by the friendships we have made, though the time involved in meeting these people often takes us away from the work we should be doing.

There were also people who came only to see the donkeys. 'Can we see Penny and Fred?' they would ask as I advanced towards them, and when they left and I was saying goodbye, they would remark as if paying me a compliment: 'Thank you for showing us the donkeys . . . *they* have made our day!'

The donkeys themselves viewed this attention with tolerant cynicism.

'Fred! Penny!' I would shout when someone had arrived, 'someone to see you!' Then again, impatiently, 'Come on, donkeys, be polite!'

They would be in sight, at the far end of the field above the cottage, munching grass with their backs to us.

'Donkeys! *Come* on!'

After a minute or so of this display of indifference, they would turn and slowly wend their way towards us, as if they were on a stage, timing their entrance to gain the maximum effect.

Photographs would follow, and this could be a tricky experience. Fred on his own was easy. He would pose his fine head this way and that, and listen with ears pricked to such phrases as: 'Isn't he beautiful? I've never seen such a handsome donkey!' But the photographers always wanted them to be taken together, and this was when the fun began. I would take charge of Fred, and Jeannie of Penny, and we would then proceed to push and shove and cajole until at last we had them facing the camera.

'One moment,' the photographer would thereupon cry, 'the focus isn't right!'

One moment!

I would cling to Fred's head while Jeannie found herself trying to hold Penny from turning her bottom to the camera. On both our faces there would be a strained look.

'Ready now!' would call the photographer. But it was too late. The subjects of the photograph were in disarray; and we would have to start the whole paraphernalia all over again.

As for Lama, she too had her theatrical moods. Sometimes she would beam friendship to an admirer, sometimes she would throw tantrums, sometimes she would simply go into hiding. She had a number of regular hideouts all of which we had plotted as if on a map. And when a request was made to meet her, I would make a round of these hideouts . . . inside the cupboard where my jerseys are kept, curled in a cup of grass on top of the heap of decaying compost beyond the far end of the Orlyt greenhouse, a round ball among the bluebells in the three corner meadow where Penny once nursed Fred, or under a doll's house arch of brambles a few feet away from the bridge where we spent summer days staring across the valley and out to sea. I would make the rounds looking for Lama, then put my hands around her and take her away from the site of her deep, comfortable sleep.

'Here she is,' I would say; and compliments would fly, and a camera click, and Lama, if she was in a good mood, would remain softly in my arms. No spicy noises of impatience, no growls.

Then sometimes I would not find her in the regular hideouts, and I would flush the area around the cottage as a gamekeeper might try to flush a pheasant. A French lady, Madame Boniface, travelled specially from Paris to meet Lama; and when she arrived Lama was nowhere to be found. Madame Boniface remained two hours, and still Lama did not appear . . . but five minutes after Madame Boniface disappeared up the lane on her way back to her Penzance hotel, Lama sauntered into the cottage.

'*Where* Lama, have you been?' I asked in exasperation; and received a purr in reply.

But Madame Boniface *did* meet Lama. I promptly drove into Penzance and brought her back; and Madame Boniface said Lama had the character of a Colette cat, and that was why she had come to Cornwall to meet her. We have been in touch with Madame Boniface ever since.

Lama, beside her regular hideouts, improvised others. These were the hideouts which frequently drove us to shout with increasing impatience: 'Lama! LAMA!'

Such improvised hideouts were always at their peak during the summer when there was a bounty of lush under-growth in which to hide. Thus Lama would vanish and we would shout for her. But I realise now that Lama, all cats in fact, revel in the moment when the slaves are shouting. This is the moment of total power over the human race.

I learnt, however, to trick Lama. When, after searching the area I had drawn a blank, I would ask the person who wanted to meet Lama, and if the person was a child it immediately became a great adventure, to steal around Minack listening for a snore. Lama was a gentle snorer, and a persistent one; and when she wasn't snoring she had a peculiar habit of making a clicking noise as she was sleepily breathing. So in silence, except for a lark singing or a black-bird and insects humming, my companion and I would steal around the neighbourhood of the cottage listening for a snore or a click. Once heard, Lama was at our mercy.

There were occasions, of course, when she took exception to being disturbed, and she would make her displeasure known in vociferous fashion, but these were the only times when she had any reason to complain. She could wake up in the morning with another lovely day ahead of her. No cars to threaten her, no dogs to chase her, always able to be her natural self; and I would watch her, and listen, as she wan-dered around on a float of purrs. She was a very happy cat.

Then one March morning I came out of my office which used to be the stables, and was faced by a startling sight.

On the near side of Monty's Leap was crouched Lama.

On the other side was a black cat.

They sleepily looked at each other; and they were both identical in size and shape.

They reminded me of book-ends.

FIVE

We were rushed, at the time, by the beginning of the peak period of the daffodil harvest. The California, most prolific of daffodils, were coming into bud so fast that we had difficulty in keeping up with them before the buds burst into unsaleable full flower; and we had much of the earlier Joseph Macleod still to pick, and the Lamorna, and Dutchmaster, apart from other varieties.

I hurried over to the small greenhouse where Jeannie was packing the bunched daffodils. It is a job that requires concentration, and Jeannie does not like being interrupted. She counts each bunch that she is packing in a box; and I often address her at these times, and she does not answer.

'There's a black cat the other side of Monty's Leap, and Lama is this side. They're staring at each other.'

Jeannie was not listening. She had to pack perhaps a hundred boxes a day; and each box had to be perfect.

'There's a black cat the other side of Monty's Leap,' I repeated.

In order to keep the bunches in place during the journey to market, a horrid metal rib is lanced into each side of the cardboard box over the stems of the daffodils; and do it carelessly and you can cut a finger. Jeannie safely completed this task on a box and then, as if she had suddenly come alive to my presence, turned round to me:

'*What* did you say?'

'Come quick,' I said, 'I believe the real Rosebud has come at last.'

Jeannie ran ahead of me, past the big Orlyt greenhouse, then through the gap into the lane leading down to Monty's

Leap. Then she stopped, and when I reached her I saw Lama strolling peacefully towards us.

'I don't see any black cat,' said Jeannie.

'It was there, I promise you. It was lying just by the gate, and Lama was this side by the violets.'

The violets were a patch of Ascania, the original Cornish violet, and I had stuck a root or two in the verge beside the lane, and they had spread. Sweet smelling on warm early spring days.

'Perhaps it was the shadow from the gatepost you saw.'

'Don't be silly. It was a black cat, and it had a head like Lama's, and it looked small.'

'Lama doesn't seem to have been upset by it.'

Lama, true, looked serene. She had reached the small lane-side well where a frog was croaking. This well, which was no more than a shallow hole beneath a great rock, was used by past inhabitants of Minack cottage during the winter. Land water collected there. But when summer came, and the land became dry, there was no water in the hole; and the inhabitants carried their pails further up the lane to another well.

Lama paused.

'Croak, croak.'

She put out a paw, a gesture full of doubt, and nowhere near the frog. The frog was out of sight, half submerged in the safety of his home.

It is sad that frogs are disappearing from the countryside. I have known summer evenings at Minack when the lane in the neighbourhood of Monty's Leap was so covered by dancing frogs that I would not walk that way for fear of treading on them. Tadpoles too abounded in the little stream from which, in the beginning of our life here, we filled our jugs with water . . . and tadpoles. Indeed on one occasion when my mother was staying with us she found a tadpole in her morning cup of tea. She was kind enough to make no fuss, and smiled away our apologies. But when she returned to London she hastened to Harrods and bought us a china contraption called a Cheavin's Saludor Filter; and thereafter we emptied our jugs into it, then returned the captured tadpoles to the stream. We still possess the Saludor, and we use it as an ornament in a corner of the garden.

Frogs, of course, are easy victims of progress. Agricultural sprays on grassland kill them, and ditches and streams where once they bred their spawn are contaminated by other chemicals. Marsh land is developed, and drainage schemes dry up vast areas where frogs once thrived. They are wanted, too, for experiments in classrooms; and so when a breeding place is discovered, earnest scholars descend upon it, and lay it bare. Tadpoles even have become fashionable, and you will find them in shops being sold at 3p each.

Fred once involved himself foolishly with a frog. Fred had a thrusting personality compared to the ruminating character of Penny. Fred, of course, has his ruminating moments just as Penny can fling away her gentle manner and be as obstreperous as Fred. Indeed she often led him astray. If they escaped from a field it was usually Penny who went first. If we went for a walk along the cliffs it was Penny we had to watch. A moment of carelessness on our part as we paused to admire the view, and she would seize the opportunity to dash past, heading for Lamorna with Fred in pursuit. However Penny was wiser than Fred, more circumspect, and she avoided the predicaments in which Fred sometimes found himself. Penny approached a mystery with care, Fred with no care at all.

Thus Penny would have avoided the incident which resulted in Fred looking so foolish. Penny would have noticed the rustling in the grass on the bank close to the small reservoir, stood there patiently observing it, and then turned away. Not so Fred.

I was standing close by at the time so that I saw the incident in detail. Fred heard this rustling in the grass, and for a moment he stood still with his ears pricked, resembling as strangers often remark, the epitome of a thoroughbred. He has a very noble head when his ears are up and his eyes alert, and he deserves all the compliments he receives. This donkey of dignity, however, was about to lose his dignity.

He pushed his white nose down into the grass . . . and a frog jumped out and sat on it.

We went back to the small greenhouse at the moment Geoffrey appeared, a jammed tight basket of daffodil buds in either hand.

'Who's been working?' he asked.

The level of wit is not high during the daffodil season. Our jokes are in mock serious tones.

'Geoffrey, is that *all* you have picked?'

'Still five baskets down the cliff to collect.'

All nonsense of course.

'Mr T.,' said Jeannie, 'swears that he saw a black cat, the double of Lama, down by the Leap.'

'It's true, Geoffrey. They were facing each other. I couldn't believe my eyes.'

'But when I got there,' interrupted Jeannie, 'there wasn't a sign.'

'Too many pasties perhaps,' he said, winking.

Pasties, for some reason I cannot remember, had become a joke word for drinks in a pub. 'Too many', therefore, meant I had seen double.

'Not at this hour.'

As it happens Jeannie and I seldom now go to pubs. We have had wonderful times in the past, and rollicking friendships. But now for the most part, a pub is an extension of some accountant's computer or a wholesaler's deep freeze; and there is always the chilling knowledge to check your enjoyment, when in fact you are beginning your enjoyment, that another happy pint will place you over the limit. Thus city dwellers have one advantage over countrymen. They can relax in their local, and make fools of themselves in innocent fashion, and have sudden friendships which may not exist in the morning.

'Anyhow,' I said, 'we'll miss the train unless we hurry.'

Jeannie glanced at Geoffrey.

'I ask you,' she laughed, 'he behaves as if *we've* held things up!'

There are two flower trains which we catch. The first,

leaving Penzance at 1.30 p.m., goes to the Midlands, and also to Southampton where we send a lot of our daffodils; and the other, at 3.45 p.m., goes to Paddington and it carries our Covent Garden consignment. Sometimes Geoffrey drives the car to the station, sometimes myself; and on this particular occasion when the Southampton train was the target, I was already in the car ready to move off when an old couple appeared asking to see me. So I stayed behind, and Geoffrey took my place.

The couple had a present for me, and by a coincidence I had had the same present given me a few weeks before at a function in Plymouth. And for the same reason. Both of the men concerned had served their time in the Tangye engineering firm at Birmingham, founded by my grandfather Sir Richard and his brothers James, Joseph and George; and having read in my books what I had written about the Tangye family, each of the men had decided to give me their only copy of my grandfather's autobiography *One and All*. I was very touched.

The Tangye firm no longer exists as a separate entity, a natural result of not being able to move with the times. Tangyes, for instance, treated their staff as members of a family. They never had a strike; and if one of the staff, shop floor or management, who had served the firm for many years, now had need of recuperation after illness, he was likely to be sent on a long cruise at the firm's expense. This generous attitude, however, was countered by the inability to make a profit; and one of the reasons for this was that the firm produced engines and hydraulic jacks of such craftsmanship that they lasted for ever. Nor during the first World War would they accept any profit for war work. Thus the firm meandered on with a reputation for high quality, but providing no money for the shareholders. In fact, for thirty-four years of my life, there was never a dividend; and if a shareholder queried this state of affairs he was considered guilty of bad manners.

My grandfather and his brother George set the standard for this liberalism towards their employees. They were the first industrialists in this country to introduce the nine hour day, the first to give a half day on Saturday, the first to pay wages on a Friday instead of a Saturday, the first to provide a canteen for the workers, and the first to provide a free health service. My grandfather also made a great deal of money but, unlike his brothers, he did not keep it. This was not due to any form of extravagance but because he was a generous philanthropist, and often a fervid supporter of lost causes. He invested, and lost, for instance, £100,000 in a Birmingham newspaper called the *Daily Argus*; and the reason for his investment was that Birmingham at the time had no journal representing Liberal views. He believed that Birmingham should have such views.

He was a great collector. He slowly came into possession of the finest collection of Cromwellian relics in the country; and he wrote a notable book about his hero and his son called THE TWO PROTECTORS – OLIVER AND RICHARD CROMWELL. He and his brother George also collected the largest collection of Wedgwood pottery in the world . . . then gave it away to the city of Birmingham.

My grandfather was not greedy in the manner of today's collectors. He did not collect for capital gain. He collected for pleasure, as a small boy might collect stamps; and having achieved his object he hoped the public would share his own pleasure. He also had strict views that national treasures should be held in their own countries.

Once, when in Washington around the 1890s, he was offered a collection of Benjamin Franklin autographed letters. The potential seller explained that he had spent a lifetime gathering the letters together, and he wanted a high price for the volumes in which they were arranged. My grandfather thereupon asked why the man had not offered them to the United States Government, adding, 'I should like to buy them, I am indebted to Benjamin Franklin's Autobiography almost more than any one book. I read it as a lad, and it influenced my whole career. But it would be a shame to deprive the United States of such a collection. Why do you not offer it to the Government?' 'I have offered it,' came the reply, 'and they say they cannot afford my price.' 'They say that, do they?' replied my grandfather, 'then go to them again and tell them if they do not buy them at once, there is a little man from Birmingham here just now, who will carry them off to England.' The United States Government found the money.

My grandfather came from Illogan near Redruth in Cornwall, where his father kept the local shop and farmed ten acres as well. His mother died when he was eighteen. Both his parents lived simple, straightforward lives, and his mother urged Richard to be the same. 'Richard, if you ever get money, never let money get to you,' was one of her remarks. 'Make straight paths to thyself,' was another. She must have been a remarkable woman in an unobtrusive way, displaying the tranquillity that is characteristic of the Quaker; and once, when cholera came to the village, she stood to face the danger while others fled. Those were the days in the countryside when good was an act of God, and evil that of the Devil. Minds had not become muddled, confused as they are now by the contradictions of a mechanical civilisation. Faith, then, was within reach.

I would have been apprehensive of my grandfather had I known him. The example set by his parents guided him throughout his life, and I would have been unnerved by his rigid beliefs. No smoking, no alcohol, no frivolous pleasures. Yet he had a dry sense of humour, and an acute observation of the behaviour and attitudes of those he met. He was a great traveller, a wandering pioneer of the industrial revolution, and a far more practical Empire builder than any politician. As a result of his journeys, accounts of which he recorded in privately printed books, Tangyes became known throughout the world.

He hated pomposity, and all those who acted a part instead of being themselves. He was brought up in the Society of Friends although he never became a member; and he was always in revolt against ecclesiastical authority. Thus he often recounted absurd stories about some of the clergy he had known.

On the way back from the States on one occasion, there was a particularly pompous bishop and his wife among his fellow passengers. One thundery night the bishop's wife could not sleep because of the heat and asked her husband to open the porthole. This he did, but on returning to his berth he suddenly saw a curious ball, attached to a wire, pop through the porthole into the cabin. The sleepy bishop first attached the wire to a nail on the cabin wall and then, after his wife complained that the ball, as the ship lurched, kept her awake as it banged against the wall, he uncoiled the wire from the nail and put the ball under his pillow. There was a severe thunderstorm during the night, and passengers next morning at breakfast described how alarmed they had been. The bishop, who had slept through the storm, described his own adventure and was delighted when the captain laughed boisterously. He was flattered to be considered such a good story teller. Then the captain told him the truth. The ball, and its wire, was the end of the ship's lightning conductor.

My grandfather had another story of a vicar he once knew who married a wealthy parishioner, a lady who brought him a dowry of £10,000 with the prospect of more in due course. The congregation knew all about their vicar's good fortune, and they crowded the church on his return from the honeymoon to welcome him back with his bride, and with their prayers. The vicar gave out a hymn which he proceeded to read instead of asking the congregation to sing it, a custom which was usual at the time. The vicar, however, had not done his homework. He had reached the fifth verse and had commenced 'Forever let my grateful heart', when he stopped in confusion, and said he would read no more. The congregation promptly looked in their hymn books at the verse concerned, and realised the cause of the vicar's distress. The verse ran as follows:

> 'Forever let my grateful heart
> His boundless grace adore,
> Who gives ten thousand blessings now
> And bids me hope for more.'

I am not sure why I have told these clerical stories of my grandfather except that, when I first read them, they made me laugh. At the same time I realise he would not like me to have laughed too loudly. I do not visualize anyone in my grandfather's company appreciating his jokes too effusively. A chuckle, yes, but not laughter.

In *One and All* he describes some of the achievements of himself and his brothers. I had a copy already before the other two were given to me, and written on the first blank page, in my grandfather's handwriting, is the endearing sentence: 'The first copy of my book! Uncorrected.' His personal corrections then follow.

And in this book he tells how these brothers from the village of Illogan designed and manufactured the Cornubia, the first 'road locomotive' ever to travel on the roads of this country. The time was the early 1860s, and the Cornubia could travel at twenty miles an hour, and could carry ten people. Its appearance was sensational, but too sensational for some who used their influence in Parliament to have an Act passed forbidding any machine on the highway to go faster than four miles an hour, with a man walking in front of it holding a red flag as well. So the Tangye brothers scrapped the Cornubia, and continued with other inventions. Their hydraulic jacks, for instance. These jacks came to the rescue of Isambard Brunel when, after building the steamship *Great Eastern*, he was unable to launch it down the slipway into the Thames. 'We launched the *Great Eastern*,' my grandfather forever afterwards used to say, 'and the *Great Eastern* launched us.' Tangye jacks also hoisted Cleopatra's Needle into position on the Victoria Embankment, and one of the jacks was placed in a recess of the base where it still lies. A multitude of other inventions came from James and Joseph, the inventor side of the Tangye Brothers team, which helped to drive forward the industrial revolution of this country. An ironic background to my life here, I sometimes think.

My father did not have Richard's flair, but he had far greater warmth in his personal relationships. He was a brilliant barrister before the first world war, but he made the mistake when victory came of staying on in the Army of the Rhine. His decision was wonderful for my brothers and myself, because we had opened up for us the world of music at the opera houses of Cologne and Wiesbaden. The performances of Frederic Schorr, Lotte Lehmann, Bruno Walter and Otto Klemperer gave us an education which resulted in a pleasure which has been with us all our lives.

But my father, I am sure, as far as his personal ambitions were concerned, made a mistake. Perhaps, on the other hand, he made the mistake deliberately. Perhaps he wanted to give us the benefit of a continental culture and, since Tangyes no longer provided him with a shareholder's income, this was the only way to do it. Both my father and mother were quite selfless in their wish to help us. It was, therefore, possible that he did this, supported by my mother; and by doing so sacrificed a legal career which would have brought him much honour.

My father, therefore, did not make use of his promise. True he held some distinguished appointments after his return from Germany, but he never had one which fully rewarded his abilities. His income always remained a low one; and he had a perpetual struggle to maintain our old family home of Glendorgal near Newquay. Richard had bought it as a holiday home, and he used to fill it with large numbers of guests during the summer. It was a big, rambling house with glorious views over Porth Bay, Trevelgue Island, and along up the coast to Trevose. But it was not an easy house to maintain, and my father used to let it during the summer, and go to live more cheaply elsewhere; and how he loathed doing this. For he had an irrational love for Glendorgal, clinging to it as if it represented the anchor of his life; and if he had to go away for three days, he did his best to be back in two. Every blade of grass he loved, every craggy corner; and woe betide the philistine who, standing beside him, failed to extol the majestic grandeur of the view.

After my father died my brother Nigel, who was then married to Ann Todd, rented Glendorgal from my mother, and so relieved her from the expense of its upkeep. Later he turned Glendorgal into an hotel, and ran it on a seasonal basis until recently when he sold it. The Tangye family, therefore, are now strangers at Glendorgal, although Nigel kept the Lodge where he now lives with his wife Moira and their young family. Meanwhile, several years before, my eldest brother Colin and I had sold our shares in the house to Nigel, along with its contents; and so he was able to develop the hotel untrammelled by our possible interference. He made it into a high class hotel with a reputation for fine food; and then slowly found there were not enough people who wanted to come to Newquay to appreciate such food, and that there were not enough suitable staff available, and in any case the four month season was too short.

I had myself, however, become a stranger to Glendorgal long before it became an hotel. Glendorgal, in my growing up, was a secret place in which I could speak aloud my thoughts, confining my doubts to the gulls as the wind blew in from the north on wintry days; and where youthful questions (how shall I behave to this girl, the first I have brought to my home?), and unformed ambitions (can I embrace life and not become its slave?), wallowed in my mind as I walked the dank, stone passages of the house, sat in the one-time day nursery, listening to the rain noisily caressing the window which stared up the coast to Trevose. I typed my first story in that room, on an ancient typewriter, and a clumsy naïve story at that; and I was hurt a little when my mother and father, after listening to the tap of the typewriter, looked at what I had written one day when I was not there in the room, and talked about it afterwards. No meanness in what they did. They were just curious as to what a son of theirs was up to who had provided no establishment proof of intellectual prowess.

I became a stranger when the war came; and Glendorgal was let to a little man who used the billiard table as an air raid shelter, sheltering under it when the rare Newquay sirens sounded. My parents then lived in a cottage on the other side of Porth Bay, and when I went to stay with them on my leaves, I used to walk on Trevelgue Island, and sit on the bouncy turf, and stare across the water at my shadows. I was never to create another shadow. I had had my time at Glendorgal. The connection was over. Only what had gone on before was to be worth remembering.

The dogs I remembered. Lance and Roy, the old English sheepdogs with whom I used to play hide and seek in the grounds because I was often on my own, Nigel away in the Navy, Colin studying to be an accountant. And there were the Maltese terriers . . . I never thought it possible at that time that I would ever be without a dog in my life. I would have been appalled if I had been told by a clairvoyant that a cat would take its place. A common cat? Rubbish. I would never sink so low.

There was first Monty, then Lama, and now . . .

We fetch our milk from Jack and Walter's farm . . . rich milk which Jeannie first scalds, and skims the surface so that we always have our own Cornish cream. We carry an aluminium can up the lane, and hitch it on a nail outside the farm gate, and Jack fills it after the next milking, usually a morning milking because that is the best one. Jeannie, on this occasion, had taken the can up to the farm one evening, and had reached Monty's Leap on her return when she too saw the black cat.

'I just couldn't believe it,' she rushed at me when she saw me, 'a black cat, the exact double of Lama. I wouldn't have believed it possible. It's Rosebud! It's Rosebud!'

I looked at her with amusement.

'A week ago I told you that I had seen it,' I said, 'and you didn't take me seriously.'

'I was too busy . . . but now I have seen it I am amazed! It is obviously a Daisy cat . . . the same shaped body as Lama, the same shaped head . . .'

It was at this moment that I had a sense of apprehension. I could not place what it represented at first and, in such a situation, one often can shrug such apprehension away. Your mood, you say to yourself, is responsible. Or perhaps the weather. You therefore console yourself by saying that

66

exterior circumstances are responsible for the unpleasant, fleeting sense of sadness. In any case, on this occasion, I kept my feelings to myself; and, instead, was outwardly enthusiastic that Rosebud at last, after the false alarms, had returned to Minack.

But had she?

It was four and a half years since Daisy had brought the little black kitten up from the cliff into the barn; and Daisy herself was dead. Where had Rosebud been in the meantime? Why had we never seen her around except for that time when we looked across the valley, six months previously, and saw the black dot in the corner of Bill's field? Why, if she had a good home somewhere, would she want to come back to Minack? She had been a frightened, unfriendly little kitten; and except for the moment she brushed against Jeannie in the dark, she had never been in physical contact with either of us. Our only contribution to her welfare, in fact, was the saucer of milk we used to give her in the barn, and which she splashed all over her face . . .

'Jeannie,' I said suddenly, 'I have an idea that will help to prove it is Rosebud.'

'I think I've had the same idea.'

'Milk?'

'Yes.'

'Then let's set the trap.'

We proceeded to do so the following morning. We were lucky. We had not long to wait. We had placed a saucer of milk in the lane on the other side of Monty's Leap when Rosebud appeared and walked cautiously towards it. We were thirty yards away by the barn with field glasses at the ready.

And when Rosebud had cleaned up the saucer and moved away, we clearly saw her face. It looked as if she had dipped it in snow.

SIX

I now started to keep a diary of Rosebud's appearances. Her visits, for a long time, had no pattern. We would see the smudge of black on the other side of Monty's Leap, then wonder where Lama might be. Lama was the Queen of Minack. Any challenger might be tolerated, but never accepted. Rosebud had better disappear again if she thought she might be able to usurp, or share, Lama's throne. There was also the question of Rosebud's sex. There began to be doubts. A significant scent was smelt on occasions, and suspicions began to be raised that Rosebud wasn't a Rosebud. But let this short extract from my diary explain our dilemma:

April 9 . . . Rosebud at Monty's Leap staring at me.

April 10 . . . Rosebud was across the Leap, and was outside the stable section of the barn.

April 21 . . . Haven't seen Rosebud for days.

May 2 . . . Rosebud back. Where on earth has she been in the meantime?

May 7 . . . Visitors came to the door, saying that they had seen Lama in the lane. They hadn't. Lama was indoors. Rosebud had played the part of Lama.

May 10 . . . No sign of Rosebud.

May 18 . . . Rosebud around these past few days, but seldom across Monty's Leap. A very nervous cat.

June 1 . . . Rosebud shows no sign of letting us touch her. We approach and she scuttles away into the undergrowth.

June 4 . . . Problems. Is Rosebud a he after all? There was

a strong smell of a tom cat by the Leap this evening. This would be serious.

June 15 . . . Rosebud has been away for some days. Then this morning Lama came running round the corner of the cottage and dashed past me inside. A second later Rosebud appeared at the corner, and I shouted her away. I've never seen them so close together before. And Lama was *frightened*.

June 17 . . . This morning I walked down to the Leap and saw Rosebud sleeping on a bank of dried grass. As usual she fled as I approached. Then I went up to the patch of grass . . . there is no doubt Rosebud *is* a tom.

The discovery jerked us into reality. We had to be sensible and make up our minds what our intentions were going to be towards the cat. We were, I realised, secretly flattered that he had chosen to hover around Minack because, after all, we never asked him to do so; and in any case we would have been pretty heartless if we had not been impressed by his apparent desire, after such a long absence, to come back to the place where he was born. Yet he had to go. We couldn't risk anything happening to interfere with the flow of Lama's life.

'We mustn't take any notice of him,' I said.

'I'll try not to.'

'We must shout at him whenever we see him.'

'That won't be easy.'

'He'll go back whence he came if we frighten him.'

'I don't want to frighten him.'

'Which is worse . . . he being frightened, or Lama?'

'You're stupid.'

'All we have to do then is to starve him. It's perfectly straightforward.'

Then I added as an afterthought: 'In any case we'll have to find a name for him . . . the days of Rosebud being over.'

Jeannie looked at me in astonishment.

'I thought you said we were never going to have anything to do with him again . . . so why give him a new name?'

'Well,' I said, 'we'll probably talk about him, won't we? So it's better to have a name which fits the sex.'

'If you say so.'

The maddening thing about the situation was that the cat had infiltrated into my mind. He had touched a soft spot, my awareness that loneliness is pitiful whether a human suffers it or an animal. Against my will I had found myself from time to time *thinking* about him; and I was moved by his perseverance which he had pursued without brashness. This black cat did not have the thrustfulness of a Felix. He wasn't barging in on our lives. He was hovering on the perimeter, watching, nervous; and, except on that occasion when he chased Lama round the corner of the cottage, he had done no harm. I had a hazy interest in the cat, like that of a man who wants to know a girl better when he shouldn't.

'So what shall we call him?' I asked.

We had been able to observe him close enough to distinguish the differences between him and Lama. From a distance, even a short distance, they looked amazingly similar, and at first glance one couldn't separate one from the other. Both had the same dainty head of Daisy their mother, and this was the reason why we thought Rosebud was a Rosebud, for it is usually easy to tell a tom from a lady. Lama, however, was more compact, and there were her extraordinary eyes which were amber, though deepened in colour by browny flecks. The other's eyes were pale yellow, and his body was thinner. There were also differences between their whiskers, and between their tails. Lama's gossamy whiskers in earlier years used to provide us with a joke form of weather forecasting because, it seemed, that whenever she grew a white whisker the months ahead were cold and wet. But now that she was growing older, white whiskers had become a permanent feature. Her tail, however, had always remained the same plush, silky plume, and it was admired by all who saw it. But the tail of the other was a miserable affair . . . it was very thin, and looked like a black, elongated twig.

'Let's call him Twig,' I suggested.

'I was thinking of Oliver.'

'Why Oliver?'

'After Mike.'

Mike Oliver was a friend of ours who kept a Cat and Dog Home near Newquay.

'All right . . . Rosebud has become Oliver.'

Oliver by now had disappeared. A week went by, two weeks, three, a month, and there was never a sign of him. It was as if he had overheard our discussions, and had decided it was better to vanish than to be scared away by our shouts. We were glad he had done so because no one could enjoy making a frightened cat more frightened; and his absence, voluntarily made, meant that we could enter again the quiet rhythm of our summer days with our consciences clear.

We no longer, for instance, concerned ourselves about Lama. She was able sleepily to wander from nest to nest without us worrying that Oliver might suddenly appear and disturb her summer thoughts. She would be absent for hours on end, and be deaf to our calls when someone arrived who wanted to meet her. This was her idea of a perfect life though, suddenly feeling adventurous, she would sometimes wander up the lane, across Monty's Leap and beyond, passing the spot where Oliver used to watch us, and continue to stroll, sniffing this tuft of grass or that, sublimely confident that she was Queen of all she surveyed. It was peaceful for us to watch her. This was the unrattled mood which we loved most at Minack.

This mood, however, had its dangers, duping us into believing that our world was full of pleasant people. It lulled us into forgetting that the rat race still existed. When we lived in London we were always on guard, always ready to try and counter the double cross if it took place. That weary war of nerves disappeared into oblivion when we came to live at Minack, until one day an American couple came for the weekend, shared a happy time, then went away and wrote a play about a Cornish cottage, which, when produced in London, was so full of libellous comments that we were forced to sue, and the play was taken off. That should have warned us for always that friends need not necessarily be friends when they came to Minack.

Yet, if you develop an attitude of distrust towards those who appear to be friends, a light goes out of life; and so it is better to be cheated occasionally rather than to be inherently suspicious. Our trouble is that we sometimes behave with such innocence. The peace of Minack is the cause of it. We become so involved in the beauty of our surroundings that we forget the world orientates around money, greed, and power. We forget that people are so consumed by the stresses of material self-survival that they do not concern themselves with ethics; and that the trans-atlantic philosophy of believing any dirty action is justified if the objective is gained as a result, is now a part of European life. We forget these things as we stare out at the view from Minack across the green bracken of the moorland in summer, then the blue expanse of Mount's Bay lined by the ribbon of the Lizard; or watch swallows sweeping the sky, or lazily listen to the bees feeding on the pink flowers of the escallonia up by the bridge or smell the scent of the musk rose beside the great rock in front of the cottage. We forget that the true values have become distorted in the pursuit of man's mania for materialism. We forget these things, and are therefore vulnerable when someone beams a false friendliness. We foolishly believe he is under the same spell as ourselves until later we discover the truth.

The donkeys have their own special moods. Fred's mood, for instance, sometimes fits him into the role of Coastguard Fred and at other times of Security Guard Fred (when he trumpets a warning that a stranger is about) or of Huntsman Fred (when he chases a fox cub across the field); and during the summer there are often opportunities to be Greedy Fred.

I am sure Coastguard Fred is his favourite role. He is fascinated by shipping, and whenever he is in one of the meadows facing the sea he is always on the watch for passing vessels. He is blasé about the regular boats like those of the Stevenson fishing fleet, though he is usually alert when the Scillonian passes by at ten o'clock in the morning on the way to the Islands. Is she on time? Does she look crowded? The same sort of thoughts may pass through his mind as through the minds of the rest of us who live on the cliffs, and watch the Scillonian week after week throughout the year. But it is the sight of a strange vessel that fascinates Fred . . . his ears are poised upright like that of the V sign, for instance, when a speed boat dares to rush past in a vacuous demonstration of power. Or when a large merchant ship, with a crew member ill or injured, slowly moves into Mount's Bay towards Penzance, then waits for the Penlee lifeboat to come out with a doctor. Coastguard Fred is intrigued by such events.

The most spectacular moment in Coastguard Fred's career, however, will surely be the occasion when the Q.E.2 paid a visit to Minack; and he was able to answer the deep, rich sounding siren of the Q.E.2 as she passed a mile or two off shore, with his personal hoots. He was hysterical with pride and pleasure, a pinnacle in coastguard watching experience; and his photograph with Penny beside him, and the Q.E.2 so close that she seemed to be touching their noses, was published round the world. The only two donkeys who have ever received a salute from such a liner.

The occasion had its beginning when the legendary Captain Warwick, first of the Q.E. captains, wrote to us one July saying that he would like to pay a visit to Minack, though he would have to bring the Q.E.2 along with him. The Q.E. at that time was calling at Cobh in Eire on her way home from New York to Southampton, and her route normally took her south to the Scillies; and so a diversion to Minack would be comparatively easy. I told our old friend Alderman Kimberley Foster what was going to happen, and he immediately decided that the event might have publicity value for Cornwall. Kim, as Chairman of the County Council for many years, has guarded the interests of Cornwall with such care that Cornishmen will be forever grateful to him. A kind man, a little deaf, though always able to hear a conversation if he wants to, he had the vision to create the great County Hall at Truro, an edifice so imposing that any visiting Government official is immediately made aware that the Cornish are a nation of their own. It was from here that Kim Foster conducted his campaign when Plymouth tried to obtain a slice of Cornwall for its own development. Kim Foster naturally won. Not an inch of any land this side of the Tamar would ever be surrendered.

Thus Kim Foster arranged that the occasion should be well covered by photographers, and he even chartered an aircraft to follow the Q.E. down the coast and take photographs as she passed each beauty spot. Meanwhile, as the time of five p.m. drew near, the time that Captain Warwick said he would make his call, doubts began to fill my mind. Would he turn up? Supposing fog in the Irish sea or some other hazard had held him up and, instead of coming to Minack, he sailed on past the Lizard to Southampton. As the photographers arrived down the lane, and the aircraft made a pass overhead, I wondered how I would deal with the situation if the evening ended with photographers but no Q.E.2. But I had other matters also to think about.

Captain Warwick had asked us to put up a signal to mark our exact whereabouts; and so we had borrowed the pole which Jeannie used to prop up her washing line, and fastened to it a gaudy orange table cloth. We then stuck this temporary flagpost between two boulders at the edge of what is now forever called the Q.E.2 field. The photographers then asked us to stand by the flagpost with each of us holding a donkey, and it was at this moment that things went astray. We couldn't catch the donkeys. We had let them loose because we believed they would become restless if we kept them on their halters too long; and I also wanted to be free from holding them because I wished to organise our personal photographs of the occasion. I realised I wouldn't have time to take the photographs myself, and so I was glad to have with us Jeannie's sister Barbara, and Richard her fiancé who had the reputation of being an expert photographer. A record of the visit would be therefore assured.

We chased the donkeys round the field, and this they

thought very amusing. They threw out their back legs as they passed each photographer, barged over a tripod belonging to ITV, and laughed their heads off as Jeannie and I panted after them. At last they were caught, new white halters were fastened on them, and all four of us arrived at our flagstaff. It was a few minutes before five.

The field we had chosen had a clear view of the sea, but it was hidden to the west by a shoulder of land thick with bracken and elderberry trees. Thus, from where we all stood, we could not see the *Q.E.2* approaching down the coast from Land's End; and we had to rely on a sentry. The sentry was Geoffrey. He posted himself at a spot where he could see the *Q.E.2* sail into view, and we agreed that he would shout as soon as she came into view. This he did, then hurried back to join us.

We waited . . . suddenly, as if she was coming out of the bracken, she slowly appeared, a mile off shore. I was overcome by her beauty, and the contrast of her modernity against the wild, primitive setting she was passing. For a thousand and more years sailing ships had passed Minack, and had been watched, and commented upon; and now this lovely liner, the last of the luxury Atlantic liners, was greeting two donkeys. The deep siren, the donkeys lashing their tails and hooting in reply . . . and Geoffrey's Cornish voice behind me :

'She would make a good wreck.'

As for ourselves, we did not have the photogenic record we had hoped for. Richard, Barbara's fiancé, discovered afterwards he had forgotten to put a film in his camera.

Not long after Oliver disappeared we had trouble that summer with Penny. Penny is a sage lady. She appears to take life rather sleepily, but she is the first to notice a movement on the other side of the valley. Her ears will prick up, and she will stare in the direction of her interest. I have learnt to respect this watchdog manner; and I will look across in the same direction, and see the head of someone, walking like a pinpoint through the high bracken. She is also a donkey of deep thoughts. Fred, although he too has his moments of contemplation, is more of an extrovert, a donkey whose life has been undisturbed by change, and who has known love since the day he was born. But Penny, I feel, has misty memories of Connemara hills, and pulling carts in bog land, and drunken tinkers, and Fred's father, and small fields with low stone hedges, and a colleen or two who put their arms around her neck; and the day she left the place where she was born, and was forced into a truck, and taken to the docks and crowded with other donkeys into a ship, the sea journey, then another long journey by truck to Exeter where she was sold at an auction, and brought to Cornwall, and a year later to Minack. Penny, I believe, is one of those who finds life sad rather than funny.

The trouble we had with her concerned her feet. We began noticing that she was having difficulty in walking and that, when she stood still, she kept shifting her feet as if she were standing on hot bricks. Her feet had always been a weakness since she first came to Minack, because of lack of attention by previous owners. Kenny, our blacksmith from St Buryan, had done much to improve them though her left foot was slightly misshapen, and it tended quickly to grow long so that she looked as if she was wearing a slipper a couple of sizes too big for her. It was beginning to look like that now, and we decided it was time to ask Kenny to call.

Kenny arrived one late June morning, and he performed his skills upon the donkeys in his customary fashion. Kenny is a patient man and a busy one, but he never complains when the donkeys behave with gross ill manners as he produces the instruments for their pedicures. The procedure is to usher them into the small courtyard in front of the entrance to the barn, then block the one exit by heaving the rusty metal slide (it was used to carry rocks away before the advent of bulldozers) that was once owned by my dear neighbour and friend the late Jimmy Williams, author of the immortal *Elephant Bill*. Once coralled, halters are placed on the donkeys, and one of them is led, sometimes pushed, by Geoffrey into the inside of the barn.

I play no part in this exercise. In fact I run away from

having anything to do with it; and when sometimes Kenny has suggested a day to perform his task which is a day that Geoffrey might be away, I hasten to tell Kenny that the day isn't suitable. I am a coward as regards this matter. I have held in my time both Penny and Fred while Kenny did his job, but I have been scared on those occasions when one of them in frisky mood has lashed out at the moment when Kenny is patiently trying to help. I then say to myself: Why should Kenny come here at all? He has more than enough to do, so why should he concern himself about two ungrateful donkeys? The answer, I believe, lies in the basic philosophy of those who make their living out of real life, instead of a plastic life. A plastic life is dominated by always seeking the easy way out, and remaining dissatisfied. A real life is rewarded by a very personal knowledge of one's own achievement. It is a reward that gives deep pleasure. It was Kenny's reward and the reward of all those who have pride in their work.

Sometimes the donkeys are docile, and on this occasion Fred behaved as quietly as a beach donkey taking a child for a ride. First one hoof was dealt with, then another, then another, and when Kenny completed paring the fourth, I heard him saying to Fred: 'What's on your mind today to be so quiet?'

Penny, on the other hand, went berserk. She lashed out at Kenny as he tried to catch a back foot while Geoffrey, holding the halter, had to use all his strength to keep her head down and prevent her from breaking loose. I would have given up had I been Kenny. I would have packed up my tools and driven away saying that I would come another day, and perhaps it would have been better had he done so. But Kenny was not going to let a donkey defeat him, and so he persisted, and gradually calmed her so that at the end of twenty minutes Penny was able to walk away with hooves as neat as a dancer in ballet shoes.

It was a Friday, and for the rest of the day I looked at Penny from time to time, and noticed she was always standing still except that she was constantly lifting one foot from the ground, then another. She was clearly in greater discomfort than she was before her hooves were pared, and this was a worry. I thought that the paring might have eased the discomfort but now, it seemed, there was something more fundamentally wrong with her.

On Saturday morning she was no better, and I thought of calling the vet, then foolishly decided I wouldn't do so because, being a Saturday, I didn't want to trouble him. A decision which, in view of what was to happen, was very foolish indeed.

In the afternoon Jeannie and I were momentarily calmed by a visit from Doreen Tovey, and her husband Réné. Doreen Tovey, of course, is the author of *Donkey Work*, *Raining Cats and Donkeys*, and other books which feature her enchanting donkey Annabel; and they are both practical people whose advice was welcome. They suggested that Penny was suffering from fever of the feet, in other words from a condition known as laminitis; and that it was caused by indulging in too much fresh summer grass. They then explained that the only way to give her relief was to fill a bucket of water, mix a tablespoon of Epsom salts in it, then persuade Penny to soak each foot therein. The first part of the cure was easy to arrange, the second part was impossible. Penny had no intention of standing with one leg in a bucket; and in the end I found the only thing I could do was to swill the water over each foot from the hock down.

We left her and Fred that night in the stable meadow. I realised there was knee high rough grass in parts of the meadow, but it was grass that had lost its sap and therefore it would do Penny no harm if she chose to eat it, which was unlikely because she had lost her appetite; and it had the advantage, when the dew fell, of providing wet corners where she could stand with the grass cooling her feet. Fred meanwhile had been showing concern during the day, and had kept close to Penny, and although this was not unusual, it seemed to me that he was paying her special attention. They were indeed devoted to each other. We never, for instance, could leave Fred in one meadow and Penny in another without an hysterical demonstration of affection. Fred would race up and down the hedge of the meadow in which he was left alone, and bellow; and Penny, though not quite so demonstrative, would react as if her world would end if Fred was not with her, and she had to face half an hour alone. Their attachment was very endearing though it seemed sometimes to me that it was so strong there was something sad in it; and that Jeannie and I were to blame. Had we been more practical when they first came into our lives, we would have trained them to expect separation because that would have been the normal, sensible procedure of a donkey owner to follow. But we did nothing of the sort. We found it less trouble to let them be, and find their own solution; and as a result I have had fears as to what would happen to the other, if they ever had to be parted.

It was a still night; and as I lay in bed I heard a badger padding down the gravel path outside the bedroom window. I could hear the hum of a passing fishing boat, and the murmuring sea in the background. An owl became talkative with another in the wood; and on the bed, curled up beside me was Lama, and when I put my hand on her there was a gentle rumble of a purr. Such peaceful sounds soon lulled me to sleep.

In my dream I heard a noise like that of a Kneller Hall trumpeter, and I was back in my early Army days.

Silence.

There it was again.

I was awake now, and it was light, and the sun was rising above the Lizard.

'Jeannie,' I said, shaking her, 'wake up, something is wrong!'

It was Fred, of course, who was trumpeting; and when I jumped out of bed I saw him at the gate of the stable meadow, and he was thrusting at it as if he was trying to get out. Then he suddenly turned round and galloped into the meadow, and he made a banshee cry, an hysterical kind of hoot, which was his habit when he was highly excited.

Away he went to the bottom of the meadow, stood there for a few seconds, then galloped at speed back to the gate. If ever a donkey was trying to give a warning, that donkey was Fred.

'Coming!' I shouted through the open window.

I ran outside in my dressing gown, and ten seconds later I had opened the gate, and was rushing into the meadow. Fred had come to meet me, then scampered away.

But there was no Penny.

I dashed through the opening which led to the barn, expecting I would find Penny inside. She was not.

I had now become panicky, and was wishing Jeannie would hurry and join me. Where could Penny have got to? And then suddenly I saw her, or rather I saw her black outline lying flat amongst the grass at the bottom of the meadow. She seemed rigid.

I was too scared to go down to her by myself, and so I shouted back to the cottage, saying I thought Penny was dead, and asked Jeannie to hurry, hurry, hurry.

Jeannie was with me now, and we ran down the meadow together, and just as we reached her, Penny moved her head, and I shouted: 'She's alive!' My behaviour might appear to have been as hysterical as that of Fred, and though I often regret my inclination to over-excitement I don't think it does any harm. A sudden temperamental explosion is usually offset by quiet thinking afterwards. And this occasion was an example.

For when we reached Penny, and Jeannie bent down and held her head she found that Penny's eyes were dim and that the eyeballs were rolling; and instead of repeating the words 'she's alive', I heard Jeannie say: 'She's dying!'

I now felt calm. Fred was ten yards away, pretending to munch grass when really he was watching us. He had done his job of waking us up. He had given us the warning; and now he was waiting for us to save Penny. I am sure he had not the slightest doubt that we would do so; and his only fear had been that he would not attract our attention in time.

'It's six o'clock,' I said, 'it's too early to phone from one of the farms so I will go to Sheffield.' Sheffield is near Paul, and I have often wondered why such a nice hamlet should have such a name. It also has a telephone box.

I hastened off there in the car, leaving Jeannie caressing Penny; and when I reached the telephone box, I was quickly talking to a sleepy vet who made no noise of objection for being woken up at that hour on a Sunday morning. 'Don't worry a moment,' he said reassuringly in his Scots accent, 'I'll be with you in half an hour.'

I returned, and we waited. A dog was barking and I was puzzled why it came from the direction of the rocks below Carn Barges, then realised it belonged to an early morning rock fisherman.

'A dog barking,' I said.

'Yes,' said Jeannie.

'From the rocks.'

'How long will he be?'

'He said he'd come immediately. He had to dress, get his car out of the garage. Fifteen minutes since I rang him. Another fifteen minutes perhaps.'

Penny, without doubt, was in great distress; and when at last the vet arrived and put us out of our waiting misery, he said another two or three hours and she would indeed have been dead. As it was, as the sun rose higher over the Lizard, and the small fishing boats of the Penzance amateur fleet set off to the fishing grounds for their Sunday entertainment, and a buzzard glided over the other side of the valley, and a lark sang, the vet injected Penny, then after a few minutes heaved her to her feet.

'Keep her upright,' he said, 'keep her moving. I'll be back tomorrow.' Then he laughed, and again the accent, 'Now for a good breakfast.'

He went up the lane in his car, bumping over Monty's Leap; and we waved.

A few yards away by the gate of the stable meadow was Fred. He scampered towards us, and when he reached us he pushed his muzzle into Jeannie's outstretched hand.

SEVEN

On August 10th we saw Oliver again.

He was a little way up the lane on the far side of Monty's Leap; and he was sitting neatly in the middle, staring down towards Minack.

My feelings were mixed. His absence had made me wonder, and worry for that matter, whether something harmful might have happened to him. Gin traps are no longer legal, but there are still the snares. Snares, in my opinion, are diabolical, and it is sad that the R.S.P.C.A. appear to approve of them. A snare can slowly throttle a rabbit or a cat; and when sometimes a cat is caught with the snare around some other part of its body, it becomes so ferocious that the trapper, instead of releasing it, kills it. I was therefore relieved by the sight of Oliver. I was also upset. We had been enjoying the old peaceful times during the past few weeks; and Lama had been able to roam as she wanted, and to continue her role as the unchallenged Queen of Minack. This return of Oliver could only interrupt her comfortable routine.

'We'll ignore him,' I said, puffing at my pipe.

'Yes,' Jeannie said, 'I certainly won't feed him.'

We were standing near the white seat with the verbena bush beside it, given us by Howard Spring when it was a seedling; and which came from the garden at Falmouth where he lived. The garden, facing the white Georgian house, with the giant turkey oak towering over the lawn, has been described by Marion Spring in her book *Memories and Gardens*, and people come from all over the world to see it. They come to see Marion Spring as well of course, and to talk to her about Howard's novels which are so readable that contemporary critics largely ignore them. She herself only became an author when she was in her seventies, and her two other books *Howard* and *Frontispiece* have been as successful as her first. This gentle, sweet person was here the other day at Minack, and I gave her a sprig from the verbena bush which once grew in her garden.

'Well,' I said, still looking down the lane, 'we can't waste our time staring back at him. We have work to do.'

We were in the last stages of the tomato season, and we were grading and weighing the tomatoes after Geoffrey had picked them. He would bring the baskets into the small greenhouse and empty the contents on to the long bench. Then Jeannie and I would pick out the very small ones and put them into one tomato box, or tray as it is called, and put the rest in two other trays, one of them being for the ripened fruit, the other for the half-ripened. Each tray had to weigh twelve pounds, and when this was done, the outside was labelled with the number of the Grade the tomatoes were supposed to represent. I have to admit, however, that we cheated on these Common Market imposed Grades. We cheated because we objected to the fact that the three Grades were only concerned with the size and shape of the tomatoes, and took no account of the flavour. Hence Grade One tomatoes might fulfil the legal conditions to perfection, yet have the taste of soap; and so we put all the tomatoes, except the very small ones, into Grade Two. Then we stapled a special card on the side of the tray which had printed in large letters: GROWN FOR FLAVOUR. This accurate description worked wonders. We were saved the trouble of specially grading the tomatoes, and at the same time caught the imagination of the buying public. Thus our wholesaler soon found he was able to obtain a premium for all the tomatoes we sent to him.

Not that this meant a fortune for us. The growing of tomatoes occupies the greenhouses in one way or another for ten months in the year. In November the soil is sterilised, and for eight weeks the greenhouse vents are shut, and nothing must be grown during the course of this time. True, we might use another sterilising chemical which completes the sterilisation within forty-eight hours, but the one we use is unpleasant enough. It has to be respected by anyone using it and its fumes can easily cause distress. But the other method of chemical sterilisation can kill. The manufacturers insist that protective clothing must be used by the operators; and that the operators must be specially trained to perform the job. We are assured, however, that the tomatoes grown from such a fiercely sterilised soil are as pure as any grown in virgin soil, though of course we have heard such optimism about chemicals before; and, though sincerely proclaimed, it has proved false. The simple fact is that commercial scientists are under pressure to produce results, and they are therefore inclined to judge their achievements on a short term basis. Only time can prove them wrong, or right, and they cannot afford to wait. I know of two chemicals that we have been confidently advised to use on our crops . . . and that are now officially banned for use in this country under any circumstances.

After the sterilisation comes the stringing. Each plant has to have its own string to climb up and, because we are busy with the daffodil harvest when the plants arrive, Geoffrey does this stringing ahead of planting during the slacker time of January. Each string of our two and a half thousand plants is attached by hand to an overhead wire, and to a small galvanised stake which is pushed into the ground after the planting. Then, during the first week of March come the plants, and the oil heating begins; and every ten days or so a mammoth Shell-Mex lorry is squeezed by its driver down our lane, and its contents pumped into the two tanks, and conveyed by pipes to the five heaters, providing us with the opportunity for the following six months to watch our money go up in smoke. All the while there is the endless pinching out of unnecessary growth in the plants which takes up many hours of hand labour; and the less time consuming tasks of opening and shutting the greenhouse vents in relation to the reigning temperature, and mixing the liquid manure for the automatic watering. Thus, when at the end of May the tomatoes begin to ripen, we have a vast amount of expenditure to retrieve before we make any profit out of our efforts.

'If only we could get a *fair* price,' murmurs Geoffrey at the beginning of a season. And what is a fair price?

I reckon that the price should average 15p a lb over the whole season, and that would probably mean an average price of 25p in the shops. Such a price would cover our costs, the depreciation on the glasshouses and so on, provide us with a small surplus for the buying of new equipment, and give us a modest personal profit, equivalent to a Bank deposit interest, on the amount of our investment. Such an average price, however, has never materialised, and is unlikely ever to do so. Housewives would revolt, questions would be asked in the House, and unions would cite it as a justification for another rise in wages. Money is for entertainment, not for food.

Yet I have no good cause to grumble. We are not being ordered to grow tomatoes. We could stop doing so, pull down the glasshouses, sell the heaters, and be spared the sight of an oil lorry ever coming down the lane again. Thus if we choose to struggle on as we have done in the past, it is our own fault. We are wishing to pretend the present situation is as it was when we began at Minack, when the prospect of possessing glasshouses and heaters promised the lure of an assured future. The trouble is that we invested large sums in this future, and we now cannot afford to give it up.

'You'll have a £2,000 turnover from tomatoes,' the Ministry adviser had told us at the time, and I had enthusiastically believed him.

He was wrong. That figure has never materialised though we have never thought of blaming him for his faulty optimism. The world has changed since he gave us his advice, and we have come to realise that we do not possess the sharp minds of business people. Our form of profit is the pleasure of living life in a slow way, amidst untamed, undisciplined, uncomputerised nature. We compromise. We have to be satisfied with trying to earn just enough to make the market garden pay.

There is, however, the other side to us, a left over from our London days. We both have luxury tastes; tobacco from Simmons in the Burlington Arcade, shoes from Raynes, wine from the Wine Society, books from Hatchards, and other foibles which have no place on supermarket shelves. Yet, when I look at the list in my accounts, each item seems to be modest, none of them wildly extravagant; and I thereupon marvel that the total is so large True, we sometimes have to go to London, but the occasions are few and far between. No gambling debts are on the list, no Continental holidays, no large-scale entertaining; and still the money has disappeared. The puzzle, of course, is commonplace. People all over the world are in the same dilemma. Where has the money gone?

I did, however, once have the opportunity of becoming a millionaire, and it was only due to lack of zest, and of courage, on my part that I didn't take it. Towards the end of the war, as I walked round London, I observed there were many streets with their buildings festooned with *For Sale* notices. In Park Lane, for instance, the lovely though bomb battered houses between Brook Street and Marble Arch looked at me as I passed, begging me to give them my protection; and I soon became so obsessed by the sight of them, by their past, and by what seemed to me to be a great future once the war was over, that I went to see the estate agents to ask the price. It was a Friday, and when I reached their offices it was twenty-five minutes to six, and the doors were shut. Had I been five minutes earlier the manager might have greeted me with open arms, and I would have been launched as a property dealer. As it was, my enthusiasm dimmed over the weekend, caution prevailed, and the houses had to wait for Charles Clore.

I have, of course, attempted to improve my bank account via the Stock Exchange. Most of us go through this stage during the course of our lives, and many of us come to regret it. In my case, my interest began when Tangyes, the old family firm, was sold to a large company and my shares, which had been valueless all my life, suddenly became worth a few shillings each. From then on the City columns of newspapers and the Stock Exchange price list became more important to me than the sports pages, or any pages.

'Get me the *Financial Times*,' I would ask Jeannie when she did her shopping, 'and the *Telegraph*.'

And when she returned, I would seize one of the papers, turn to Engineering on the Stock Exchange price page, and cry out : 'They're up!' Or throw the paper on to the floor, murmuring : 'They're down.'

This continued for many months, even a year or two, until I began to realise that my excitement was based on a void. When I strode out to Geoffrey in a confident mood after I had read the shares had gone up by 5p, I was behaving like a small boy in a nursery game. I had been hypnotised by the city jargon of newspapers. I really believed I was growing richer when all I was doing was having fun. After all, a 5p rise was a myth unless I sold the shares.

The period I am remembering was a 'bull' period. Everything was going up. City people became so excited, and so confident, that they invented names for Trust shares like Growth Units. Everything was growing. Support Growth! And then one September day, the *Financial Times* open before me, I woke up to reality. My Company had dived 30p.

I was now to become aware of the problems that face stockbrokers. Everybody loves them while the market is going up, and they bask in reflected glory like racing tipsters enjoying a good run. They appear to have such a deep knowledge of economic affairs that outsiders like myself convince ourselves that we only have to follow their advice for our fortunes to be assured. Alas, we are foolish to do so. Economic affairs are not controlled by economists, or stockbrokers, but by a force as mysterious as that which controls the wind.

Thus for no reason that the pundits could agree upon, the 'bull' period turned into a 'bear' period; and my Company shares fell and fell and fell. 'There's too much money in circulation,' said one distinguished pundit on a television programme . . . 'Too little,' said another sitting beside him. Then the rasping voice of a union leader intervened: 'On behalf of my members I want to say you're both wrong . . .'

As for myself, the day came when I was advised to sell my Company shares. 'Spread your capital in other companies,' I was told. I obeyed; and soon afterwards the shares of the new companies dived down, and those of my old Company leapt up. Too late for me.

Oliver continued to haunt Minack, and we continued to ignore him. It was not too difficult to do so because he never, until one day in late September, crossed to the cottage side of Monty's Leap. He would sit for hour upon hour beside the granite post of the white gate, staring up the lane as if he was willing us to pay him attention. He certainly was not begging for food, so he was no doubt having enough from somewhere. Yet what compelled him to come to Minack despite our rebuffs?

He was now such a fixture on the other side of the Leap that we became careless about Lama; though she herself seemed content, showing no fear of him when she wandered down to the stream and saw him on the other side. She roamed the immediate area of the cottage as she always had done, settling in long accustomed nests, sleeping in a curled black ball, Queen of the world she had known so long. But visitors were confused.

'We were coming down the lane, and we were very lucky. We saw Lama! We took a picture of her.'

'That wasn't Lama.'

'Oh?'

'No, it wasn't Lama, it was . . .'

I soon gave up explaining who Oliver was. It was too complicated. Nobody would believe or understand me. And anyhow I didn't want to talk about him at the expense of Lama.

'That was not Lama,' I would say therefore, 'that was her understudy.'

The answer silenced some but not all.

'What do you mean by understudy?'

'I think you will find the explanation towards the end of my book *Lama*, the story of three Christmases here at Minack. You'll find out about the understudy, about the little kitten we found down the cliff.'

At the end of September, however, the understudy caused serious trouble. We had taken the donkeys a walk along the cliffs, and down the road to Lamorna and the pub. Once upon a time, when the Bailey family presided at the pub as if they were hosts at a party, we used often to visit the Wink, as the pub is called, and the donkeys much enjoyed the potato crisps which were offered them. Then the Bailey family left the pub and, because we felt we would never again have the natural fun we used to have there, we gave up going. We are not regulars now, but occasionally, and this was one such occasion, we walk to the pub, have a glass of beer and feed the donkeys with crisps.

On our return we left the donkeys in the stable meadow, walked through the wooden gate which has divots in it because the donkeys gnaw at it when they are bored; and saw two black cats staring at each other a few feet apart close to the white seat.

'Don't move,' I said to Jeannie, 'let's see what happens.'

It was absurd how alike they were, except for Lama's compactness and the tails.

'Perhaps they're going to be friends,' said Jeannie.

'I doubt it.'

Their eyes were unblinkingly staring at each other, and I was reminded of a game we played at Copthorne, my preparatory school, called the stare game. Two small boys would stare at each other and the loser was the one who dropped his eyes first. Then the winner would take on another small boy and another, until he was declared champion starer of the Form.

I am afraid Oliver was the champion starer on this occasion. Lama suddenly turned and bolted up the path, then disappeared around the corner of the cottage.

'Damn,' I said.

Lama was scared, though Oliver had not moved. Lama, Queen of Minack, had panicked on her own territory. Oliver had imposed his personality upon her, and I was angry.

'Shoo,' I said, advancing towards him, shuffling my feet on the chippings so that I made a noise like a tyre spinning. 'Shoo,' I hissed, 'shoo, shoo, shoo . . .'

And Oliver raced down the lane.

'Good riddance,' I said firmly.

The incident, as it turned out, was of benefit to Lama. We often used to leave her out at night until we were ready to go to bed, and then we would bring her in. Sometimes in winter she was out for hours, and we would not bother what might be happening to her. She was capable of looking after herself. Born a wild cat she was accustomed to the adventures of the night. She had never caused us concern. Rain, snow or a howling gale, we took it for granted that she was able to look after herself.

But what we had forgotten was that she was growing old. Three years before she was quick enough to catch a stoat, and mice galore, and a rabbit or two. Now, we realised, she had eased off on her hunting, and she was sleeping more, and contemplating more; and in any case she now ran away from an intruder.

A few evenings after that incident, I was standing by the bridge having a drink when I heard a cacophony of cat-like screams down by the Leap. It was dusk, and I could see nothing from where I was, though I immediately jumped to the conclusion that Oliver was causing trouble again. Lama loved to take an evening walk down by the side of the Orlyt greenhouse, through our small orchard to the gap in the hedge where the stream runs and which is framed by the elm trees and which leads into the main glasshouse field. Lama loved to walk this way, then turn right past the compost heap to the lane, and back to the cottage across the Leap. Sometimes she would stroll one way, sometimes the other, but the route was always the same.

I put down my glass on the slate ledge which serves as a

table on the bridge, and ran down the lane shouting like a Dervish on the attack. I was finished with Oliver. We hadn't asked him to come to Minack. We hadn't fed him for weeks, we owed him nothing, and yet he was completely upsetting the rhythm of our days.

Just as I reached the Leap I saw Lama on the other side in the shadow, and it wasn't Oliver I saw crouched close to her, spitting. It was a large grey and white cat with a small head, and big ears which looked like those of a fox. It reminded me of pictures of the devil. It didn't stay a second when I arrived.

So I had been wrong about Oliver. I was glad. He may have been upsetting our routine, but he had never given the impression of being a fierce cat. On the contrary there was something forlorn about him as if, like a lonely person, he was looking for love. At the same time he *might* attack Lama, and we were certainly not going to risk this happening, nor a repeat of the attack by the grey and white cat; and so from then on Lama was kept indoors as soon as dusk fell.

I also decided that the time had come to take more seriously the question as to where Oliver came from. We had lazily let the question lie fallow because it did not seem all that important; and we also did not want an answer to the question which might cast doubt on our firm belief that Oliver was the original Rosebud. Yet it was nearly six years since Daisy brought her black kitten up from the cliff and deposited it in the barn. It must have found a home somewhere . . . was it possible that after the ten days' stay in the barn, Daisy took it away again and left it at one of the farms nearby? An extra kitten among a farm population of cats and kittens might not be immediately noticed.

We already knew he did not come from the two farms at the top of the lane, the Rosemodress farms, and we therefore decided to ask the owners of Tregurno when we next saw a member of the family. The family, the Jeffrey family, were old friends of ours though, despite the fact the farm was only a mile and a half across the fields in the direction of Lamorna, we seldom saw them. When first we rented

Minack, and before it was habitable, we used to stay at Tregurno, a splendid old Cornish farmhouse with front windows facing farm fields, moorland and the sea; and it has today a fine reputation as a farm guesthouse.

The Tregurno farm, at the time, used to take their milk churns to the milk stand at the bottom of the lane, on the edge of the main road; and there they were daily collected by the milk lorry and taken to St Erth, the site of the milk factory. One morning, when I was driving into Penzance, I arrived at the milk stand when young Roger Jeffrey had just unloaded his churns. Roger was a wandering spirit of the countryside, and I would often see him in the early morning striding along with his dogs, gun at the ready, hoping for a rabbit. Nothing wrong in shooting a rabbit, but how he hated snares! Strange to see a young countryman feel so strongly about something which others took for granted.

'Have you ever had a black cat your way?' I said, stopping the car beside his tractor, winding down the window. He leant forward from his seat, a good looking Cornish face with black hair.

'You mean Blackie? Oh yes, I've seen him down your place from time to time. All the others at the farm go for him. I don't know why. He's the odd one out.'

'I can't understand why he comes down to see us,' I said, 'we don't encourage him, in fact it's the opposite. We want him to go.'

I had stopped the engine of the car but the tractor's engine was still ticking over, and it was difficult to hear what Roger was saying. Then I added, and it was, I afterwards realised, the sixty-four dollar question: 'How long has Blackie been with you?'

'Nearly six years,' said Roger.

It was nearly six years since the kitten had disappeared from our barn.

'Thank you, Roger,' I said, and drove off.

I felt vaguely pleased. I would not have liked him to have said: 'Oh yes, that's our Blackie . . . he's only two years old.' That would have spoilt the game. I wanted to continue to believe that the black cat and the kitten were one and the same; and I was therefore suffering from conflicting emotions. One part of me was enjoying the mystery of a cat who wanted to return to his original home, the other was wanting to be free of his persistent attention.

A while later I saw Roger's mother and I brought up the matter again. Mrs Jeffrey was a great cat lover, and I remember Jeannie returning once from a visit to Tregurno, brimful of cat mania enthusiasm for the well fed cats warming themselves against the Aga.

'That's our Blackie down your place,' said Mrs Jeffrey, 'no doubt about that . . . you feed him I expect?'

'We haven't for ages.'

'He comes back to us for a day or two, then off he goes again. I've even tried shutting him up in a room, but it doesn't do any good. I'm very fond of Blackie.'

The mystery became more puzzling. Why should a well fed, well loved cat, ever wish to leave its home for the sort of treatment we were giving him?

'Perhaps he goes,' went on Mrs Jeffrey, repeating what Roger had told me, 'because the others attack him. They don't seem to like him.'

I then put to her the idea which had long been in my mind.

'We had this kitten which disappeared from our barn,' I said, 'and it was about the same time as your black kitten of Tregurno. You don't suppose Daisy, the mother, carried it across the fields to your farm, just as she carried it up from the cliff to the barn, and for some reason left it with a foster mother with kittens of the same age?'

Mrs Jeffrey couldn't accept this. She was sure she knew the litter in which Blackie was born.

'I just wondered,' I said, 'whether the others attacked him because they knew he didn't belong to the Tregurno cat dynasty.'

We both laughed.

'Anyhow,' I added, 'you can be sure we're not trying to keep him.'

The situation had now become more complicated. Oliver, in his original name of Blackie, was yearned for by Mrs Jeffrey to go back to Tregurno. Oliver, in the role of his Minack name, had this mystical desire to haunt Minack. Lama would like to see him gone for ever, and Jeannie and I agreed with her . . . until we caught the look of Oliver staring at us up the lane. Then we couldn't help sensing that there was some curious magic being performed. Heavens, at this stage, we had no notion of its meaning. There was nothing logical about it. Only a mood, like the scent of a flower on a summer's evening one cannot place.

The rains came at the beginning of November. We were thankful for them. The level of our well had sunk so low that we had been rationing ourselves. The local Water Board had offered to put us on the mains, at a price, but we had refused because the enchantment of our well was that it gave us water like that of a pure mountain stream. We might go short at times, but the inconvenience was worthwhile. We were free from the taste of reservoir water.

We were also free from what Jeannie describes as the country's Achilles heel. Her silly idea is that the most vulnerable part of the country's fabric lies in the reservoirs open to the skies in all parts of Britain. She suggests, in Orwell fashion, that an enemy could drop quantities of chemical into these reservoirs which would result, as the water passed through the mains, in all those gulping a glass of water from the tap, either dying, or going to sleep, according to the wishes of the enemy.

She also has a more amusing idea. A British Government might make use of the reservoirs. The Government wants to condition the public into accepting some normally unpopular policy. The reservoirs are dosed with the lulling potion, and the electorate, sipping their cups of tea and quenching their thirst, perform in docile fashion in exactly the way the Government had planned . . . except for the well drinkers. The Government's computer had not allowed for them. They are alert. Their minds are razor sharp. People, therefore, like ourselves, discarded by the bureaucrats as the outcasts of reservoir society, save the country. It's funny, except it might prove true.

The rains fell, and Oliver did not mind.

He made himself a niche in a pile of old grass and bracken trimmings which was heaped beside the lane just beyond the Leap and the white gate. Above it were the bare branches of an elm and a May tree, and they gave him little shelter. His shelter, for what it was, was a small umbrella of bracken covering the dent in the grass on which he curled. He might be there for two or three days, then away for the same period; and if we walked up the lane he would lift his head and stare at us as we passed, an intent though timid stare.

At the beginning of December I found him lying there at night, and, though the sky was clear, a gale was howling through the trees, and a small branch fell in front of me as I walked. His unusual faithfulness had begun to get on my nerves. We were conducting a war with a cat who refused to be defeated. There we were ignoring him, refusing to feed him, and yet by a Gandhi-like meekness he was putting us in the wrong. Now, having seen him lying there at night, I began to doubt whether our toughness was justified. Something compelled him to behave in this manner, what could it be? I had no answer to this at the time, though I felt the moment had come when he might have a reward. One had to be pretty heartless to ignore such remote control devotion and, provided it did not interfere with Lama's life or stop him from returning to Tregurno if he wished, it didn't seem foolish to offer him again a saucer of milk.

Jeannie laughed when I suggested it.

'After all these weeks of sanctions, you give in!'

'Sanctions never are of any value,' I answered, 'if the opposition is determined.'

So Oliver had his milk again, and again dipped his face in it, as if he was eating the milk and not lapping it. And more important, of course, he rejoiced in his victory.

Not that he embarrassed us by displaying affection. He ran away when Jeannie advanced up the lane with the saucer, then only would reappear when she had gone. First a saucer of milk, then as Christmas drew near, a saucer of fish, or chopped meat. But Jeannie still had to leave it on the ground, as if she was leaving it for a wild animal, then disappear before Oliver would dare to come out from his hiding place.

Soon he had another victory.

'There's an old wooden box in the barn,' Jeannie said, 'and if I put it down there near where he's sleeping, and put some straw in it, he'll have some protection from the weather.'

Oliver moved in the same day without any encouragement from us. He was there on Christmas Eve, then absent during Christmas Day, but back at nightfall when Beverley Nichols paid a call on him.

Wise, witty, self-deprecating Beverley was spending the daytime of the holiday with us, though staying at an hotel in Penzance. He had, of course, a devotion to cats which was similar to that of the Egyptians in the time of the Pharaohs. His attitude, therefore, was in tune with that of Jeannie and so, when they were together they indulged in that kind of cat worship which I still find a little distasteful. I will give an example.

I took them for a drive in the car around Zennor, Gurnards Head, Morvah, Pendeen, Trewellard and St Just . . . and I had to be ready to pull up and stop whenever they saw a cat which caught their fancy. At Trewellard, for instance, there was a huge tabby sitting on a garden wall, sitting peacefully, eyes half closed, when he was suddenly awoken from his dreams by Beverley and Jeannie jumping out of the car, hastening towards him with arms outstretched, and cooing those curious noises which are peculiar to cat worshippers. The tabby, however, I have to admit enjoyed it. He was still being rocked in Beverley's arms when the startled owner appeared, and by chance he was the coalman who delivers our anthracite. 'My friend,' I said nervously, 'loves cats. He writes about them, you know.'

On the other hand there are also cats which do not succumb to these extravagant blandishments; and Lama was one of them. Lama liked to maintain her dignity. Lama did not favour those who threw flattery at her as if it was confetti, and then expected her to yield submissively to their wishes. Hence, when after the Christmas lunch Beverley expressed a desire to rest and invited Lama to share his bed, I doubted whether the union would be a success. Lama, for instance, squeaked when she was picked up from the sofa and carried into the bedroom, notwithstanding Beverley's protestations of devotion. And when the door shut on the bedroom, I wondered what kind of rest Beverley would enjoy. Ten minutes later I had the answer. The door was opened a few inches, and Lama flew out.

'They have had words,' I said to Jeannie.

That night an easterly was blowing, and we put on coats before walking down the lane to visit Oliver in his box. I carried the torch, Beverley a saucer of chopped turkey, and Jeannie a saucer of milk. Oliver was about to have a feast, and we only hoped he would be there.

He was there all right. I shone the torch towards the box, and lit the pinpoints of his eyes. But would he answer our calls? Would he respond to the most inveigling noises that Beverley and Jeannie could devise? Certainly not.

Like Lama, he was immune to flattery.

EIGHT

The first daffodil was in bloom by the middle of January; and by the beginning of February we were gently picking a basket or two. This was the most pleasant part of the daffodil season. The rush hadn't started, expectation existed; and as always Lama came with us as we wandered among the meadows close to the sea.

She would walk up and down between the beds, the black plume of her tail mingling with the green spikes of the daffodil leaves; and sometimes when I was bending down to pick a stem, she would come to me, pushing her head against my hand, and then I would cease to pick, and proceed to pay her the attention she expected of me. Or I would put a basket down at the edge of a meadow, go on with my picking, then look back and find her sitting in the basket. Or suddenly I would see her alert, stalking a noise in a bank of young grass, the sea as a background, a gull floating overhead, a robin observing from a branch. Moments like these made a mockery of the far away world where fanatics throw bombs for narrow causes, where politicians manoeuvre for personal power, where strikers bellow defiance at reasonableness out of boredom, where earth moving machines destroy a thousand years of history in an hour. Moments like these place the jargon of words like 'rationalisation', 'productivity', 'growth', 'monetary crisis', 'differentials', 'price index', and 'progress' in their true perspective. Such moments offer the Grail which man seeks.

'All life,' I said, 'except this instant is a dream.'

'Why do you suddenly say that?'

I was standing in a tiny meadow which borders an area of blackthorn within which are the homes of both a fox and a badger family. One of the most desirable sites in Cornwall, we say, because they are safe from the humans who would like to kill them. Jeannie was beside me; and Lama was squat at our feet, black tail round her paws, swaying her head, utterly at peace.

'Well,' I answered, 'what do you remember of this morning?'

'I got your breakfast, the post came, I wrote a letter to my sister, I wrote half a page of my book...'

'All hazy now in your mind.'

'I suppose so.'

'That's what I mean. Half one's life is dreaming of the future, the other half dreaming of the past.'

'I understand.'

'Our sophisticated years are now a dream, all the times at the Savoy, a bottle of champagne on ice in our room, a first night . . . Cholmondeley House, Thames Bank Cottage, glamorous parties in your office with Danny Kaye and all the others. Only the instant was permanent.'

'Like now.'

'Yes . . . you and I and Lama, and that robin, and the gull sailing down into the bay, and that wave moving in to smack the rocks . . . this is the instant which is real.'

Jeannie laughed.

'And now it's over!' she said.

I was being too serious, and she was bringing me back to my senses.

'All I was meaning,' I finished by saying, 'is that one mustn't take these instants for granted.'

The wind began to blow that evening, coming from the south, first the scudding clouds, then a spitting of rain, then a torrent. It is a pleasing experience to be in a Cornish cottage with feet thick stone walls, listening to the elements roaring and screaming, pausing to take breath, then at it again, tearing at the old granite weathered by ages of such storms. There is the atmosphere of cosiness, and safety, and the marvellous sense of being attacked by forces outside man's control. A storm is a sign of my freedom. In the final instance I can laugh at a militant, an economist, a television commentator or a leader writer. They can mouth their opinions about how I should conform to their theories . . . but I am free. The rain and the gale sigh and shout and fling their strength against Minack, and faith is restored. The cockiness of humans is in perspective.

I lay on the side of the bed nearest the door so I was favoured first when Lama decided to jump on the bed. She jumped up and nestled close to me, and I woke up, suddenly finding her presence; and when I put out my hand and touched her, her purrs joined the roar of the gale and the rain. I lay there in the dark with my hand cupped round her; and I found myself wondering about Oliver. I felt a twinge of guilt. I was being unfaithful. There was Lama beside me, blissfully confident in the affection she was receiving, while my mind revolved around her rival. Where was Oliver in this storm? Was he safe in his box down there beyond the gate? Similar twinges of guilt are felt by errant husbands and wives when, although keeping up the pattern of normal behaviour, they are thinking of another.

There was no easing of the rain and the wind in the morning. The cottage windows are small, too small for present day building laws, and so when the clouds are low it is dark in the sitting room. It was very dark that morning, and we had our breakfast with the standard lamp switched on.

'Lucky,' Jeannie said, 'we don't have to worry about the daffs. Another fortnight and we might have been in trouble.'

'What are you going to do today?'

'First I have to make bread. There is only a crust left and I'll give it to the donkeys. Then I'm going to try to finish my chapter. That will be six.'

'Half way.'

'I am so slow.'

I am too. I envy those writers who spill words on to paper with the speed of sand poured from a bucket. If I write five hundred words in a day, I am ready to celebrate. Such a celebration, however, is rare.

'I read the other day that Arnold Bennett wrote five thousand words of *The Card* in two days . . . then retired to bed with a migraine for three. It was a week before he was ready to write again.'

'I would put up with a migraine,' said Jeannie, 'if I could do that.'

I had finished my breakfast, and I went over to my desk and picked up a pipe and filled it. But I paused before I lit it and looked at the rain lashing against the window, the window from which I could see the barn and the lane leading down to the Leap.

'I think,' I said suddenly, 'that before I do anything I will go and see how Oliver is getting on.'

'I'll come with you . . . I'll take him the fish that Lama's left.'

We put on our yellow oilers and went outside, and down the lane; and as I did so, I glanced at the stable meadow and saw in the far corner the donkeys with their bottoms to the hedge. Heads down, mournful, yet I knew that nothing would move them from their positions. They enjoyed their masochism. They would remain there, despite the warmth of the barn which awaited them, the rain drenching their winter coats, until Jeannie brought them that crust of bread. For a minute they would then become alive. Then back they would return to their lugubrious manner. They were martyrs of the weather. They made certain we realised it.

We reached the Leap, and the stream was a yard wide and gushing towards the sea; and we half jumped to cross it, and a few yards on we came to the spot in the copse beside the lane where Oliver's box was placed, and found it awash.

'Idiots,' I said, 'we should have remembered this gully was sometimes flooded.'

No sign of Oliver. No sensible cat, in any case, would remain in a place where there is no shelter. If Oliver was wise, he might have had dreams of a nice warm Aga, and given up his siege of Minack. That would have suited me. I would like to be rid of my twinge of guilt.

'I'll leave the fish here in any case,' said Jeannie, her voice almost inaudible in the noise of the storm.

'Better not, it'll be drowned in the rain.'

So I took the saucer from her, and we started back to the cottage.

On the other side of the Leap, a few yards up on the right and close to the little land-well which is covered by a stone canopy and where past inhabitants of Minack once filled their pails during the winter, is a gorse bush. It is a large gorse bush with gnarled branches and dense prickly foliage, and in early spring it has a resplendent display of yellow, scented blooms.

We were about to pass it when we heard a miaow. A sharp crack of a miaow like the sound of a rocket fired from a boat in distress.

We both darted to the gorse bush . . . and there was Oliver crouched on a wrist wide branch three feet from the ground.

'Oliver!' Jeannie cried out, and I added, 'Couldn't you have found a better place to be in this weather?'

He could have done. He could have gone back across the fields to Mrs Jeffrey's Aga.

'Funny cat,' said Jeannie.

'I'll put the saucer down here.'

He sat on the branch staring at us; and I knew if we went any nearer he would flee away.

'I'll make you another house,' I said solemnly, 'and I'll make it above high water.'

Later in the day I proceeded to build it. I gave it a foundation of rocks and a covered entrance. On the rocks I placed a new large wooden box, then roofed it with polythene, and filled the inside with hay. The whole was camouflaged with old bracken, as if it was a thatched cottage. It was a splendid house, and this prompted Jeannie to make a joke, saying that Sir Christopher Wren could not have done better; and so Oliver's new home was christened the Wren House. He was delighted with it, and he moved in the same evening; and he continued to use it for several weeks until an injury prompted him to move.

In the meanwhile came the daffodil season; and the daffodil season that year was enhanced by the presence of Fran. Fran was an Australian girl from Burnside, Adelaide. She was just twenty-one, fair and small, sturdy, affectionate, occasionally moody, indefatigable and very willing, and had a wonderful way with Geoffrey.

'Get a move on, Geoffrey,' would sound the Australian accent as they went out together to pick daffodils.

'It's just not good enough, Geoffrey,' would come the Australian accent again, 'you shouldn't leave things hanging around like that!'

Fran was on a working tour of Europe. She had been in this country a few weeks and had a job in the Co-op in Reading when her sister, with whom she was staying and who had come to live with her husband in England, proposed that she should write to me. They had read a book or two of mine. Fran wanted to see Cornwall . . . and she preferred the outdoors to a shop counter. So the two of them concocted a letter to me; and before I had time to answer it, Fran one Sunday morning arrived at our door.

'Couldn't wait,' she explained, 'to find out whether you wanted me.'

She had arrived in an ancient two seater car, and she had driven from Reading, and it was January, and the forecast that morning said heavy snow was on the way. I said she was welcome to work during the flower season, and we fixed a date when she should come, and I said I would ask Mrs Trevorrow whether she could stay with her.

'In fact I'll ask her,' I said, 'whether you can stay there tonight. You can't drive back to Reading with snow coming.'

'Oh yes I can.'

She spoke defiantly. Why is it there are those who grate when they speak their mind, while there are others who give no offence? I took Fran's attitude without concern.

'See you on February 21st,' I said.

'Sure.'

We sent her into the Lama field the first day she arrived, to pick Joseph MacLeod. The Lama field was a new acquisition, a rented acquisition, and it had a curious history as far as Lama was concerned. The field was almost as close to the cottage as the donkey field from where the donkeys looked down upon us when we were in the porch. It was adjacent to the bridge where we had our meals on summer days, and for years it had been cultivated by a neighbour. During all that time Lama never went into it, tempting though it must have been for her to do so. Yet the very day after it came into our possession she was wandering around it, inspecting it, like any new owner of a property; and as we watched her we decided that we would call it the Lama field.

Fran preferred picking daffodils to bunching them, and after the first few days she proved to be a very quick picker. She would arrive in the morning with a small hold-all slung on a stick over her shoulder, the hold-all containing her lunch, personal odds and ends, and cigarettes. For an outdoor girl she smoked far too many cigarettes.

'It's wrong I know, Mr T.,' she would reply when I remonstrated with her, 'but I'm a nervous type, strung up.'

Off she would then go to join Geoffrey, and from time to time we would hear peals of laughter if the meadow in which they were picking was near; and we would be thankful that the flower season was going to be a happy one.

On the big daffodil farms the daffodils are picked *and* bunched in the field. I never understand how this can be done satisfactorily, but the reason for doing so is the paying of labour by piecework. Finding labour to pick flowers becomes more difficult every year, and piecework allows a big grower to employ all and sundry without losing money on some of the types who come. Yet there are physical difficulties about bunching in the open which I find impossible to surmount, and Geoffrey agrees with me. For instance, if there is a howling gale and rain, how do you slip a rubber band on a bunch of ten blooms without it taking a minute or two fiddling to do so? And how, with such amateurs involved in the piecework, can you guarantee that each bloom in the bunch is perfect? The truth is that with the arrival of some big growers from up country in Cornwall, the standard of daffodils sent to market has dropped. Often poorly bunched, always crammed too tight in a box, such growers have helped to reduce the price received for daffodils; and in any case they are not interested in flowers. Their main interest is the marketing of the bulbs.

We ourselves have pride in each box despatched, and we have an unfashionable kind of pleasure out of doing a job, though sadly underpaid at factory standards, which will give people happiness. Thus it is vital not to have any harsh element during the flower season which will bite into our enthusiasm. We may only have two or three extra helpers from time to time, but they all have to love their work. A sulky intruder spoils everything.

Fran, occasionally, was sulky, but she was never an intruder.

'Geoffrey, Mrs T. and I, like you,' I said after a week or so, as a way of teasing conversation.

'You're joking!'

By that time, although I did not know it, she had decided to paint the inside of a small hut that stood in one of the meadows, erected years before, and used for 'shooting' potato seed; and where later I had sat, writing *A Gull on the Roof*. She had an hour for lunch, and instead of spending part of it with Geoffrey she would disappear. It never occurred to me what she was doing until I discovered it by chance. I passed by the hut one morning, decided to look in to check that all was well . . . and found to my astonishment that the inside had become rejuvenated. Instead of the work-a-day, dismal, cobweb-ridden interior, there was a sheen of fresh brown paint on the walls and ceiling.

'Why didn't you tell me?' I asked Fran.

'Surprise, Mr T.'

'But the cost of the paint . . . you can't possibly afford it.'

'How do you know?'

'It's obvious. You wouldn't be here if you could.'

'That's a beaut.'

'Why?'

'You don't know anything about me, Mr T.'

I was to know enough that we were all sorry when the flower season came to an end, and she left to go on a solo exploration of Britain; and we made sure that she came back to us during the summer for a month to help with the tomatoes and the digging of bulbs.

NINE

Meanwhile Oliver appeared to be enjoying the Wren House, and he displayed increasing signs of losing his nervousness. Jeannie, for instance, on several occasions had succeeded in stroking him. No longer had she to drop the saucer on the side of the lane, then run and hide behind the hedge of the greenhouse field if she was to watch him emerge and consume her offering. He now did not mind her standing beside him in the lane. We observed also that he had a companion, a robin, who watched him constantly from a branch a few feet above his house, though he himself took no notice of its presence. We therefore wondered whether like Lama, and Monty, he did not chase birds.

A week after Fran had left to go on her travels, I looked one early morning out of the bedroom window and saw Oliver near the white seat. The sight of him so close to the cottage was a surprise, though it was not this that caused me to call out to Jeannie. What prompted me to do so was that he looked to be in trouble. He was hobbling on three legs. His back two legs were sound, so also his right front one, but the left one was dangling. I watched him hobble out of my view in the direction of the garage.

'Oliver's had an accident,' I said, 'he's cut his foot.'

'How?'

'You'll have to examine it.'

'He'd never let me.'

I paused.

'I know. I'll get my field glasses, and we'll see if we can

focus on the damage ... and we might get a clue as to what has happened.'

When we went outside we found that Oliver had gone into the garage, and had curled up at the far end beside the front wheels of the Volvo upon an old sack. I couldn't possibly train my field glasses on his foot. It was obscured by the car.

'We'll have to wait for him to come out,' I said.

I realise, in retrospect, that this was the turning point in our relations with Oliver. Up to now we had kept him at bay. We had treated him with goodwill though in distant fashion. We had succeeded in pursuing a policy of moderate kindness without taking upon ourselves any responsibilities. Our role had been that of do-gooders who were anxious not to become involved. But now our role was about to change.

Oliver slept all morning on his sack, and it was not until after lunch that he appeared again, hobbling on the chippings. I fetched my field glasses, and stared. For a half minute I had the chance of seeing the trouble quite clearly. There was a deep cut on his left paw, and the fur of the paw had been rubbed away. An inch or more of it was bare to the skin.

'A snare, Jeannie,' I said, 'I guess he's been caught in a snare.'

We afterwards joked that he deliberately caught himself in a snare in order to gain our sympathy. He certainly received such sympathy, and he responded as any grateful patient might be expected to do. Instead of the frightened cat we had hitherto known, he meekly accepted Jeannie's nursing; and he displayed no objection as, twice a day, she bathed his paw. The cut was deep, and he must have struggled for some while, before he was released by the arrival of the trapper. If a cat is in a snare for a length of time, this length of time can be an advantage despite the physical suffering; and the reason is that the cat is exhausted when the trapper comes, and he doesn't struggle. But a cat, newly caught in a snare, can behave so ferociously that the trapper may not attempt to release it. He just knocks it on the head.

Jeannie bathed Oliver's paw every day for a week before he put it to the ground again; and she bathed it with Exultation of Flowers which comes as a liquid or a cream. This potion originates in Nairn in Scotland at a place called Geddes, and the creator of the potion is Alick McInnes. We always keep a bottle both of the cream and the liquid for ourselves, and the same for any sick animal or bird. The liquid, for instance, is also remarkable for the way it restores a stunned bird, or a bird who is suffering from shock. I remember a merlin crashing into the garden (it was after a dunnock), and it looked like a boxer being counted out until Jeannie opened its beak and forced it to accept drops of the liquid; and then it quickly revived. Chaffinches, thrushes, blackbirds, even a green woodpecker have all received the benefit of the liquid, victims of the greenhouse, the glass of which they did not see in their flight. And what is Exultation of Flowers? The description on the bottle suggests an old wives' tale brought up to date:

> Electrical impulses in stable suspension, obtained by potentising the following flowers by an entirely new method and in harmony with cosmic radiations:
>
> Oak, Eucalyptus, Water Crowfoot, Sunflower, Bean, Daisy, Birch, Mimosa, Dandelion, Violet, Rose, Larch, Vetch, Marigold, Gowan, Bulrush, Dahlia, Gladiola, Tulip, Hyacinth, Pansy, Spiraea, Heather, Gorse, Broom, Aconite, Daffodil, Larkspur, Cornflower, White Clover, Red Clover, Wallflower, Forget-me-not, Pentilla, Viburnum, Syringa, Olive, Lotus, Bluebell, Coreopsis, Periwinkle, Mesembryanthum, Pink, Carnation, Iris, Mathuiloa, Fig, Star of Bethlehem, Ageratum, Petunia, Mustard.

This, of course, is not a miracle potion. I have, however, witnessed some remarkable results; and it certainly helped to cure Oliver.

Oliver now proceeded to move from the Wren House and

take up his headquarters in the garage. Doubtless he had been impressed by the care Jeannie had bestowed on him and he sensed it would be foolish not to make use of it. She had not only looked after him but, more important still, she had shown affection. Thus he had won three victories since the initial rebuffs in his campaign to return to Minack . . . saucers had been put down for him beside his adopted home beyond the Leap, the Wren House had been built for him, and now at last he had experienced the first signs of the love he wanted. No wonder he decided to move closer to the cottage.

Thus he now introduced another crack in the routine of our life at Minack. He hadn't brazenly intruded as in the case of Felix but had instead infiltrated out of gentle persistence. It was a maddening situation. Deep down inside me I remained anti-cat, and yet I had to admit to myself that my anti-cat defences broke down whenever an individual cat chose to entice me with its charms. First, Monty, then Lama; and now here was Oliver hovering on the brink. It vexed me that I should have been put in such a situation. It vexed me that my loyalty to Lama should be challenged. Why couldn't Oliver abandon his pursuit of us? Why couldn't he return to the comfort of his Aga?

He had no intention of doing so.

'Don't let Lama out,' periodically I now had to call to Jeannie, 'Oliver's round by the water butt!'

Or:

'All clear. Oliver's up the lane.'

As the summer went by there were periods when Oliver continued to disappear, sometimes for several days on end; and we would be relieved by his absence, and once more become forgetful about him, and Lama would take up again her natural routine.

He was, for instance, absent during the week a BBC 2 television unit came to film us for a programme in the Look Stranger series. The unit was spearheaded by the camera team of the *Troubleshooter* stories, and the director was a small attractive girl whose husband was an important personality on the BBC catering side. His importance, and usefulness, was apparent when, in the course of the filming, there was a day devoted to Fred's birthday party, and he provided the cake. All the children of St Buryan were present, and they marched down the lane towards the donkey field where the party was being held, shouting: 'Happy birthday, Freddie!' They arrived at the field where Fred and Penny were waiting, then gathered around the trestle table upon which the director's husband had set the large BBC baked cake decorated with red marzipan carrots and green marzipan apples. Jeannie led Penny up to it while I led Fred, and before we could stop them they stretched forward their heads and ate both carrots and apples. It was very funny; and their performance was greeted by shouts, clapping of hands, and child-thrilled cries of applause.

Ironically this pleasant occasion belonged to the same period during which some of the occupants of St Buryan were misguidedly used by an American film company to feature in *Straw Dogs*, the most unanimously condemned film of violence any film critic had ever known up to that time. The film company, however, most generously compensated all those concerned, including the children, and so everyone was satisfied except those worldly souls who realised that *Straw Dogs* was another nail in the coffin of those who put their faith in integrity.

Oliver's absence from Minack during this week helped to ease the task before us. It was unnerving enough to wake up in the morning knowing that we had to try to appear pleasant, intelligent and pictorial, without also worrying whether Lama might have an involuntary meeting with Oliver.

There are of course those who blossom on such occasions, and I envy the confidence they display. Jeannie and I have been involved in a half dozen television programmes, and each programme has produced its moment of terror. The first occasion was when Alan Whicker came to Minack. We had no television set then, and so I did not recognise him as he stepped out of his car, a dapper figure with highly polished black shoes. I advanced towards another man, tall and impressive, instead: 'Good morning, Mr Whicker,' I said. It was the cameraman. Several hours later Whicker and his team departed from Minack; and we went to bed until noon next day.

There was another programme in which we found ourselves standing on a cliff near the Lizard, each of us with a hidden mike, a camera trained upon us, then told by the director to talk casually to each other. We carried on like this for five minutes, then the director who was in the television van way up on the top of the cliff, waved us to stop. I paused for a moment, and thinking that the mike was now dead, I said: 'Thank God for the gin!' Laughter thereupon, pealed down the cliff side.

Nevertheless television helps to sell books. Yet, in this pursuit of book sales, one must be on guard against becoming too involved in the publicity machine. Publicity is necessary when a book is newly published, but after that lie low. Some authors, however, leap at any opportunity to make a speech, forgetting the maxim that authors should be read and not heard. They find it enjoyable, for instance, to open fêtes, speak at literary luncheons, Women's Institute gatherings and those of other organisations. But as for myself I run away from public speaking unless I have no alternative; and then I stand on a platform, stare at the up-turned faces, and feel unreal. A mass audience is not my scene. Writing, for me, is a secret affair; and if what I write is read, it is because the reader and I are in sympathy with each other. It is a personal relationship. Thus I have no desire to stand on a platform in the role of a public entertainer because I long ago discovered that my inhibitions prevented me from being an actor.

I was therefore at a natural disadvantage in one scene in which I was supposed to talk *ad lib* into the camera. I was sitting on a garden chair with my back to the escallonia, and the bridge to the left of me. Cameramen, the sound man, and the director were facing me, three or four yards away on the patio which is covered by an umbrella of blackthorn. My idea was to put forward my theory that anyone today who intends to give up town life and go to live in the country should first take courses in bricklaying, plumbing, gardening, carpentry and any other vocation which would give him practical independence. However, each time I started my dissertation I forgot what I was going to say after a minute, and my mind went blank. The director would then try to coax back my confidence.

'Now, Derek,' she would say, smiling sweetly at me, 'Look at *me* while you're talking.'

The trouble was that Derek received no inspiration at all by looking at her; and charming and delightful though she was, I remained tongue tied. I thought of the scores of people in my life to whom I had been able to babble without effort . . . and now on this important occasion I was dumb. There had been similar occasions in the past nevertheless, women whom I have wanted to enchant but with whom I have been silent. Years, years ago, and I still remember them.

'Now, Derek, we'll try again . . .'

It was not until the autumn that the programme was shown on BBC 2, and as it was in colour Jeannie and I proceeded to rent a colour television set which was delivered on the morning of the day concerned. This was a mistake on our part. We should have had it delivered days before, so that we could become accustomed to the knobs and the various strengths of colour and light which they control. We sat side by side, the room in darkness, the screen before us . . . and there we were. We looked awful. We were the colour of oranges.

There is a postscript to the programme which needs telling. I was up there by the bridge, stuttering out my words concerning my theories as to how those who want to leave town life should prepare themselves for the country, quite unaware what was going on behind my back. The director was murmuring: 'Now, Derek . . . ' but behind me on the blue slate of the bridge was Lama; and she was calmly, exquisitely, washing herself. She stole the scene.

Fran breezed back into Minack in the middle of June.

'Guess who I found on the John o' Groats shingles?'

'Can't guess.'

'Two Aussies!'

She had careered around Britain, up the east coast and down the west, in her little grey car, living on bacon sandwiches.

'Didn't you ever get hungry?'

'Why should I?'

That sprawling Australian accent, earthily real.

'Any adventures?'

'Ran out of cigarettes between Carlisle and Keswick.'

'Am delighted.'

In retrospect I don't think we really needed her help. One can so easily make jobs for people unless one is on guard.

Geoffrey could have picked the tomatoes without Fran. A lot of bulbs would also have been dug. But we would have missed the gales of laughter, or the sudden silences.

'What's wrong today, Fran?'

'Mrs Trevorrow gave me too much breakfast.'

'Better than too little.'

'That's what *you* think.'

'Still don't see why she did wrong.'

The small figure turned towards me.

'I'm slimming, see?'

The arrival of the postman was an event of enormous importance for her. Like many a distant traveller, however content in their passing environment that they might be, she was homesick at post time.

I would meet the postman and there was an air mail letter from Adelaide.

'Fran!'

She was with me in an instant, to seize the letter, and hurry away with it, like a crow with a trinket. A while later, I would ask what news she had had from home.

'Haven't read it yet.'

'Oh,' I would answer, remembering myself when on a

world tour, caressing a letter from home until a secret, suitable moment.

At the end of the month, she went off to join the Vyvyan family at Trelowarren, one of the most beautiful estates in Cornwall. Amanda Vyvyan is my god-daughter to whom I dedicated *A Cornish Summer*; and we were of course responsible for Fran going there. The day before she was due there came a crisis.

'I'm not going,' said Fran.

'Why?'

'Not in the mood.'

'You'll let us down, you know.'

'Shall I?'

'Yes.'

'Oh well,' she said, and the Australian accent seemed more pronounced than usual, 'I suppose I'll have to.'

Just as well she did. Or am I wrong in thinking that? She was introduced into a new kind of life at Trelowarren, and she loved it. She came into contact with a far wider social world than she had ever known before; and as a balance she was able to enjoy the quiet loveliness of an estate which belonged to centuries of time. She was a great success at Trelowarren, and sometimes she would come over to Minack with Amanda.

'Come on Mr T., be sociable.'

At the time I was writing a book, had put my typewriter away at half past nine in the morning when they had arrived, had spent morning, lunch, afternoon and tea with them, and then heard her say: 'Be sociable, Mr T.' But it was her birthday and so I forgave her.

She left Trelowarren to look after the child of a rich couple in Paris, then the child of another rich couple in Switzerland. There was a visit in between to Spain; and letters to Minack.

She is now back home again in Burnside, Adelaide; and we had a letter last week from her: 'My regards to Geoffrey. I often think of him, and wonder if he has ever smoked a cigarette since last I saw him . . .' At the end of the letter there was a special message for Jeannie: 'Want me to clean the silver, Mrs T.?'

During her stay with Mrs Trevorrow, Fran reported seeing Oliver up by the farm from time to time. His absences during the summer had been fairly frequent though they never lasted for more than a day or two; and Fran's information gave us the clue as to what he was up to.

He was attracted to one of Walter Grose's many lady cats who maintained their crêches in various corners of the farm buildings. Periodically, however, the kitten population became so large that Walter, kindhearted though he was, had to enrol the help of the R.S.P.C.A. to dispose of them. These periodical clearances no doubt caused much maternal anguish, and it would seem that the more experienced mother cats would sometimes change their routines, and have their families away from the farm buildings where they could not be found. This, I think, is what happened in the case of the lady cat who was particularly favoured by Oliver.

I first saw them together one afternoon in late summer, a few hundred yards down the lane between the farm and the main road. They were sharing a gateway into a field, Oliver at the hinge end, his lady at the other; and there was a gentle, adoring look on Oliver's face which showed no change when I called to him from the car as I passed. The lady was not pretty. She was brown, black, grey, white, with a slash of orange across her face; and, though I believe most people would pass her by, Oliver was enraptured. Several times afterwards I saw them together, and the mood between them was always the same. They were deeply in love.

At the beginning of October I saw the lady at the Minack end of the lane, close to Monty's Leap. I am sorry to say I hissed at her. I also shuffled my feet hastily on the gravel so that the noise frightened her, and she ran away. Oliver was causing trouble enough without also having to cope with his girl friend. After this incident she disappeared, and I did not see her again.

In the middle of October, however, an event occurred

which is one of the strangest I have ever known in my life.

It was a Sunday morning. Jeannie had taken the car to St Buryan to post letters and collect the Sunday papers; and after she had left I had strolled down the lane to Monty's Leap.

Oliver suddenly appeared as I stood there and, with the confidence he now had gained, came up close to me. As he did so I heard a tiny cry in the undergrowth to my right from the direction of the Wren House. An instant later I could not believe my eyes.

A tiny ginger kitten, the exact colour of Monty when he was a kitten, stumbled out of the autumn leaves which had gathered beside the lane.

And Oliver ran towards it, and began immediately to lick it.

TEN

I left them together, Oliver licking the kitten as if he was the mother, and hurried up the lane. Jeannie would soon be back, and I had to stop the car before she reached the gate, and tell her what had happened . . . and warn her that we would have to get rid of the kitten forthwith.

'Stop!' I cried.

I had reached the well, half-way up the lane to the farm when I met her. She looked bewildered. I had never before confronted her and the Sunday papers in such a fashion.

'Bad news?' she asked anxiously.

'Terrible news,' I replied, 'Oliver has brought us a kitten.'

The engine was ticking over, Jeannie's side window was down, and I was appalled to see her face mellow into gentleness. No sign of shock. No sign of disapproval; and I realised I had been an idiot to expect from her any other reaction. Her record provided enough evidence that she wouldn't be on my side.

She switched off the engine, stepped out of the car and said: 'I'll walk very quietly, not to disturb them.' Then added: 'What is the kitten like?'

Her question could have been parried if the kitten had been a tabby or some other colour which had little significant distinction. Had this been so I could have laughed the matter off. I could have said that Oliver had produced a kitten out of the undergrowth, and I had frightened it away. 'Oliver ran off also,' I might have been able to add. But the kitten was ginger, and it had miraculously appeared close to Monty's Leap, so how could I dismiss the matter casually?

'Well,' I replied, 'it is a very odd situation. There I was standing with Oliver by the Leap when there was a miaow from the undergrowth just beyond the gate, then out on the lane appeared this tiny ginger kitten.'

'Ginger?'

'Yes, ginger. That's the extraordinary thing.'

As it happens I never called Monty ginger. I described him, after I had first met him playing with a typewriter ribbon on the green carpet of Jeannie's office at the Savoy Hotel, as the size and colour of a handful of crushed autumn bracken. I could have described Oliver's kitten in the same way. I didn't do so to Jeannie because it might have suggested enthusiasm on my part.

Then she saw the kitten.

We had reached within twenty yards of Monty's Leap, and there in the shadow beside the lane were the two of them. The kitten was nudging Oliver.

'It's Monty!'

The damnable part of the situation was that I couldn't argue with Jeannie. The kitten *was* Monty as I remembered him as a kitten. The little white shirt front, a smudge of orange on each paw, a tail with dark rings against cream, the rings graduating in size to its tip. There was only one difference, and an important one at that. Monty, on that afternoon at the Savoy Hotel, immediately set out to woo me by endearing antics. His double, so many years later, behaved in exact opposite fashion.

As we approached, he fled.

I was thankful. It is easier to be tough if affection is not being used as a weapon against you. Monty tried to climb up the inside of my trousers, Lama came to the door in a storm, Oliver wanted to come home to Minack . . . such demonstrations of wishing to know me dented my obduracy. I yielded.

But a kitten which was as wild as an autumn leaf had no claims on me, and though I had to admit that the circumstances were extraordinary, I believed on that Sunday morning I would be able to deal firmly with the situation.

'Now Jeannie,' I said, 'we have to think of Lama. No soppiness on your part.'

My tone was a mistake. I sounded aggressive, anticipating a mood which I knew was there but which was not yet on display.

'I'm not being soppy.'

'I know you're not, I didn't mean that, but you know how you *can* be . . .'

'*You* found the kitten, *you* were standing by Monty's Leap . . . I wasn't.'

My intentions were good, but I had manoeuvred myself into being in the wrong. This can easily happen. One slip, and the other is at you. You try to retrieve yourself, make a counter-blast, and before you know where you are, there is an argument over a matter quite different from what you began with.

Jeannie went back to the car, and I walked on to the cottage. All my fault, I said to myself. It's always the same . . . I object to the arrival of a Monty, Lama, Oliver, Penny, or a Fred, and am then proved wrong. It is as if I am trying to cling to an independence which fate no longer intends me to enjoy. I splutter my objections, give in to Jeannie, and am pleased in due course that I have done so.

I arrived back at the cottage as she drew up in the car. She was laughing.

'You *do* get unnecessarily worked up sometimes,' she said.

A remark I could not deny.

'My apologies,' I said, making a mock bow. Then jokingly added : 'Nevertheless I'll leave you if you feed that kitten.'

I had never envisaged the time when Lama would grow old. Lama, I foolishly thought, would always be with us. I never doubted it. And yet concern now began to creep into my mind. Attempts were being made to intrude on her life which were beyond normal understanding. First Oliver, now this kitten. She was no longer free in the way she had been for all her years at Minack. We had to be her sentries and her scouts. We were guarding her so that she would think nothing had changed. We were pretending. We wanted to pretend that Minack was her domain as it always had been since that day she cried at the door in a storm.

Yet no one was deliberately trying to oust her. I have known people ousted from their businesses, from their farms, and from their homes. I have known people buy another dog or a cat because they were frightened by the age of those they already had. But in Lama's case no one was trying to oust her. Lama, we both believed, was immortal, no substitute was wanted. A comfortable feeling, had it not been for Oliver.

Oliver watched, hung around, and waited. What was going on in his mind as he stared at us? Did he realise that Lama was growing old and he was young? And what was it which prompted him to produce a ginger kitten from the undergrowth so close to Monty's Leap? There was no logical explanation for the coincidence. This was a magician's trick. It was uncanny. And although I had made my customary noises about keeping the kitten at bay, I knew in my heart that if it played its cards correctly I would not be able to send it away. First Oliver, now the kitten. Both uninvited. Both a threat.

For three days the kitten remained on the other side of the Leap, and we would watch it playing with fallen leaves in the shadow of the trees. Then on the fourth morning, I found Oliver in an unusual mood. Instead of keeping at a distance I saw him advancing towards me from the direction of the white seat and the verbena bush. Then he self-consciously turned on his back, in the manner of Lama's endearing habit, and with legs in the air he watched me coaxingly with his yellow eyes. I took no notice, whereupon he jumped up, rushed past me and disappeared under the car in our so-called garage. It was then that I saw the kitten. It was asleep, curled on a patch of old straw between the wall and the rear wheel. I did not disturb it and went into the wood to see Geoffrey. When I returned, the kitten had gone.

I had, a few weeks before, created a bedroom for Oliver in the shelter where we kept the tractor. It was a large card-board flower box laid on two boards several feet from the ground. I had lined it with hay, placed the lid of the flower box at right angles so that it served as a draught proof wall on the open side of the bedroom, and left an opening above the packing case containing greenhouse spare glass from which he could jump in. It had met with his favour. It met, too, with the kitten's favour. The following morning, instead of its being on the floor of the garage, I found it in the shelter in the bedroom; and Oliver had a black paw lying across its tiny body.

It was very young, so young that its eyes had not yet changed their colour, and they were still blue; and one would have thought it still required the attention of its mother. However it seemed happy enough snuggled up to Oliver, and I left them together to go and fetch Jeannie. When we returned, they both had vanished.

We saw Oliver again that day but not the kitten, though the following morning the kitten was once again snuggled up to Oliver in the bedroom. This time, however, we were more circumspect. I only glanced at the two of them, then Jeannie placed a saucer of bread and warm milk flavoured with sugar close to the wheel of the tractor; and we then both retreated to the shed opposite, where Geoffrey sits when he has his meals. We watched the kitten jump down from the bedroom, then dip his face in the saucer. This moment, I thought, was an excellent moment for a photograph; and so I stepped out of the shed, pointed the camera at the kitten, and clicked. The print showed the blur of a running ginger kitten.

There now began a frustrating period during which the kitten made it quite plain that it did not want anything to do with us. It ignored Jeannie's blandishments, except to consume the contents of the saucers offered. This was no cuddly kitten. This was no kitten saying to itself how wonderful to be welcomed by members of the human race. It intended to be free, from the toddler stage onwards. 'If you are idiot enough to feed me, and give me a bedroom,' it seemed to be saying, 'that's all right with me . . . but I don't owe you anything.'

Nevertheless it owed Oliver something. As the days went by, and the kitten kept aloof from the attention we were ready to offer, its attachment to Oliver was touching. We also observed, from a distance, the behaviour of Oliver in the role of an anxious, loving parent . . . taking the kitten on walks, slapping its face when it became cheeky, and watching carefully when it wobbled off on an adventure of its own. The kitten in return plainly respected Oliver. It realised that though it might treat Jeannie and myself with disdain, it had to obey Oliver. Oliver, it seemed, was one of those old fashioned fathers who was able to impose his personality on his offspring.

The kitten, after a few weeks, had to be given a name; and as Jeannie is a natural name giver I left the task for her to do. The first step was to discover whether it was male or female; and so, since it was impossible to catch it during the daytime, one night we stole down to the shelter with a torch. I put my hand into the bedroom, seized a wriggling ball of fur and held it up while Jeannie investigated. It was a boy.

'Ambrose,' exclaimed Jeannie almost immediately, the torch still shining on him, 'we'll call him Ambrose!'

'Well,' I said, letting him escape from my hand, 'what a very odd name for a kitten.'

'It's simple,' she explained illogically, 'when the torch lit up his face it softened the ginger colour of his fur, and it looked amber. Then his little face made me think of the amber musk rose in the garden, and so I put two and two together and there's the name Ambrose . . . Amber-Rose. See?'

We were walking back to the cottage, and she couldn't see my face in the dark. I was smiling tolerantly.

Later I was to learn of another Ambrose, a St Ambrose who lived in Italy in the fourth century. He was a distinguished lawyer who became a Roman Catholic priest and a great preacher; and he took special pains to attack the dogma of the Roman Catholic church that animals have no souls, that man alone is a spiritual being. This dogma, he believed, resulted in great cruelty being inflicted on the animal world; and he preached a series of sermons which have recently been republished in Italy urging his hearers to treat animals with kindness, and as part of the oneness of life.

I know quite a few people who should be forced to read these sermons and learn them by heart. People, for instance, who discard dogs and cats when they are bored with them, as casually as if they were empty cigarette packets. People who set snares at random, or use similar devices to catch birds. People who hoard wild animals in confined spaces on land, in ships, and in long distance aircraft. People who spray chemicals indiscriminately, turning the hedgerows brown and killing the wild flowers, the butterflies and harmless insects of the countryside. People who persecute badgers, badgers which were here before man arrived. People who dupe themselves into believing that the human race has a divine right to exploit nature. People who are leading future generations to live in a cement-covered Britain where the only animals will be in zoos, the only green spaces in municipal parks.

Thus the name of Ambrose has some significance. It is not so silly as it seemed that night when Jeannie christened him.

A westerly gale blew the bedroom in the shelter asunder at the beginning of December, the wind bashed the flower lid flat which was serving as a draught proof wall, and shifted the flower box which served as the bed, as well. And so we decided that Oliver and Ambrose should have two bedrooms . . . the one in the shelter which was cosy when the easterlies and the southerlies were blowing, and another in the small greenhouse where we bunch our daffodils in which they would be safe from the westerlies and the northerlies. This greenhouse bedroom also had other advantages. Both Oliver and Ambrose took a great liking to the two hay filled boxes we provided for them . . . and they were content, therefore, to be shut in there for periods during the daytime; and this meant that Lama could then wander at ease around Minack.

It was easier to shut in Oliver than it was Ambrose. Oliver we now could pick up without much difficulty. Ambrose was so elusive that we could never come within a few feet of him. We had to lure him into the greenhouse, bribing him with whiffs of freshly boiled fish.

There was of course no harm in Ambrose, but we set out to keep him and Lama apart because we did not want her to be annoyed by such a juvenile newcomer. There was another reason too. Ambrose had such devotion for Oliver that he became distressed when he could not find him. It was better for them to be shut up together.

The day came, however, when we could not find Ambrose, and Oliver was shut up on his own. Ambrose had set off on an adventure soon after breakfast, and we did not see him again till lunchtime. We were sitting on the white seat, the verbena bush beside us now bare of its scented leaves, and Lama lying like a pocket Trafalgar lioness a yard or two from our feet.

Suddenly Ambrose appeared coming under the donkey nibbled gate in front of us; and he proceeded to make a pathetic mistake. He came scampering towards Lama, a loving kitten smile on his face and an eager readiness to nudge head against head. But instead of the welcome he expected, he was greeted by first a threatening growl, followed by a hiss which sounded as if a long suppressed steam engine had found its release. Ambrose raced away. For the first time he had discovered there were two black cats in his life.

This incident fortunately did not leave its mark on either of them, and indeed Lama was to become intrigued by Ambrose. A few days later Ambrose came walking up to her under the elder tree in front of the barn where she was sitting upright, like a cat replica of Queen Victoria. Ambrose may have mistaken her for Oliver again, but I think not. He had learnt his lesson. His approach was not so bold as on that first occasion, suggesting he realised that here was someone who deserved a well mannered respect.

'Hello Auntie,' he seemed to say, then walked on.

He was however to find, as time went by, that Lama could be unpredictable. He might offer to greet her with a friendly nudge of the head, and receive a short hiss as a reward. He would then look surprised, hasten away, pause and look back. What had he done wrong? But there were other times when Lama would watch him as if she was mildly amused at the sight of him discovering the world of Minack . . . Ambrose trying to catch a moth in the dusk, Ambrose becoming unbalanced on a branch and holding on with his front paws, swinging like an acrobat, Ambrose looking up at Penny and Fred as if he was thinking they were mountains on the move. There was no friction between Lama and Ambrose. Her attitude was one of tolerance, the attitude of the elderly to the young, and she was only gruff with him if she thought his ebullience was taking her for granted.

I wish I could say the same of her relationship with Oliver. She was frightened of him, and we no longer could pretend otherwise; and although most days we were able to keep Oliver out of her sight, there were inevitable confrontations. They would then have their staring matches. They would be several yards apart, crouched, and I would not dare to intervene in case I set a light to a fury between them. Instead I would watch, and will Lama to win the staring match, or better still try to will them both miraculously to break off the match, and be friendly with each other. But the match always ended the same way; and suddenly Lama's nerve would break, and she would turn and flee back to the safety of the cottage.

There was one moonlight night shortly before Christmas when Lama wanted to go out, and I escorted her up to the Lama field. Across the bay were the sparkling lights of Porthleven, and the flooded lights of Culdrose, and those of the upturned mushroom dishes of Goonhilly pointing towards their Satellites. A glorious, keen night, salty sea air to breathe, a myriad stars winking above me, and silence. No passing boat to break the silence, no aircraft screaming, only the murmur of waves on rocks and the sudden coughing bark of a dog fox to remind me the natural world was continuing as it has done since the beginning.

Lama was ready to return, and so in the manner of a Special Branch man guarding the Queen I scouted ahead, down the two steps from the field to the bridge, then left with the huge *escallonia* on my right, and down past the waterbutt to the door of the porch. At the side of the waterbutt is a bush planted a few years ago and now so large that it hides the waterbutt. A splendid windbreak, and scented in summer with tiny bells of white flowers. Underneath it, the shadow is very dark; and as I went past I did not see Oliver sitting there. Thus Lama, hastening back to the warmth of the indoors came face to face with him, and there was an explosion, and after that they scattered, and I couldn't find either of them.

We found Oliver first, and he gently let me pick him up and carry him into the greenhouse. But there was no sign of Lama, and for an hour or more Jeannie and I searched the area, calling, calling . . . in the wood, back in the Lama field, down the path to Fred's field, up the lane beyond the Leap. Lama, Lama, we called, and became every minute more worried. Not that, as it turned out, we had any need to feel worried. We had reached a stage of near desperation when, with the moon pencilling the finger branches of the orchard trees, Lama approached us . . . nonchalantly, mistress of the occasion, a Queen who put her Special Branch man in his place by her dignity.

ELEVEN

Jeannie and I were on our own at Christmas; and when Geoffrey set off at lunchtime on Christmas Eve to have fun with his family, we opened a bottle of champagne and toasted the holiday to come. No decisions to make, an embargo on trying to solve problems, no cause to move away from the environment of Minack. This was a sweet moment. The world would peal its bells, the people worship in their churches, and boisterous bodies would dance and shout, wearing paper hats and throwing streamers, and television programmes would yell their jollity; but here it would be quiet. Clouds skimming over the Bay, a gull crying on the roof, a magpie chattering in the wood, a fan of wind breathing through the trees, a woodpecker laughing at dusk, and the sea murmuring, always the sea murmuring.

'What are you going to do with Oliver and Ambrose this Christmas Eve?' I asked Jeannie.

'We might give them something special in the greenhouse bedroom.'

The greenhouse bedroom had its door kept ajar, a tiny entrance large enough for Oliver and Ambrose but small enough to deter intruders. It was a better place for a Christmas Eve banquet than the muddy floor of the shelter.

The donkeys always had mincepies on Christmas Eve, munching them one by one in the barn after we had tantalisingly held each mincepie in front of their noses for a second or two; and they munched in the light of a candle softening the ancient, rough granite walls, grey white with limewash. Lama, meanwhile, the saucer in front of the fire, would be rejoicing in the turkey giblets; and this was a routine that both donkeys and Lama had been involved in year after year.

'What special something?'

'I've got a John Dory.'

John Dory was Lama's standard fish until it became too expensive, and she became accustomed to ling instead.

'They'll like that.'

We went down the cliff after lunch. We have a holly bush growing there in a corner overlooking the sea; and though it never produces berries, the curly leaves are dark green and spiky, and they look well decorating the cottage; and so, as we needed another armful to complete the decorations we set off to collect some. We hadn't walked a dozen yards down the path to Fred's Field when I looked back and found Lama trotting behind us.

A Lama walk was both an honour and a comforting pleasure. An honour because it was her own personal, secret decision to come with us, and a comforting pleasure because of her antics . . . the sudden spurt ahead, the wait until we caught up, the dashing off again at the very moment I stooped down to stroke her. It was comforting, too, because the three of us were on our own again, far from any possible interference by Oliver and Ambrose; and it was specially comforting to have such a walk on Christmas Eve, for we had shared many memorable Christmases together. I had, too, a reason for this one to be perfect. I had a restless, niggling feeling that this one would be her last at Minack. I was to be proved wrong, proof how foolish it is to be swayed by menacing premonitions.

We reached the bottom of the field, and she rushed in front of us under the small gate at the top of the cliff, and down the steps, and through a little meadow where the pointed foliage of the Magnificence daffodils were already showing in rows. We followed, and as we did so a band of Long Tailed Tits took off from the fuchsia hedge to our left, a score of them perhaps, and they flitted away towards the blackthorn which covered the cliff to our right. Only in mild

9

winters do we see Long Tailed Tits, restless, tiny pink cushions; and in a hard winter they die as easily as the red-wings which sweep down from the north in search of warmth and then, when not finding it here in the far west of Cornwall, career up the south coast, north again, dropping away all the while from the main stream to die in snow covered coverts and frost hard fields, until there is no main stream left.

'We're lucky,' I said.

'Lucky, lucky.'

We paused by the little cave where first Lama, then Oliver was born. It was not really a cave. It was a gap between two great rocks, and the narrow top was covered by a mass of ivy so that it was dark inside, and dry.

I laughed.

'I wonder how many times we have spoken that word,' I said.

'Thousands!'

In a world in which so many people are chained to routines they detest, or waste the hurrying days of their lives protesting against imaginary injustices, or conscientiously live their years but fail to fulfil their youthful dreams, it is sensible to appreciate one's luck.

I am always touching wood. We both are. We have had long periods of failure in our lives; and so we are always on guard. Many occasions when expert advice has led us astray, or we have made stupid misjudgements, and debts have mounted as a result, far exceeding our bank balance. I am always remembering these financial terrors, and the long, early morning wakes which came with them.

There was the depressing period after I had submitted *A Gull on the Roof* to a literary agent who never read the book himself but informed me that his reader had given a most disappointing report about the manuscript. We were broke at the time and I had been clinging to hopes of a quick acceptance. Then at last the agent said he had found a publisher who would accept it, a minor publisher ... and the agent had so bruised my confidence by his comments that

I was in danger of agreeing. It was during daffodil time, and I paced up and down the flower house with daffodil bunches in my hand wondering what to do. A funny sight in retrospect. Should I accept and thus be certain of paying the garage bill? Or should I refuse, and hope I could find a publisher among the top class of publishers? It was indeed a dismal period. The daffodil season proved to be a bad one; and when I finally turned down the minor publisher, months went by before the manuscript found the home I wanted. Then, after the book was published and it had some success, this publisher gave a party at Claridges to celebrate the twenty-fifth birthday of the firm, and kindly pressed us to attend as special guests. We were unable to accept. We had too many debts. We hadn't the money to pay our fare to London and back.

'What is it,' I said to Jeannie, my eyes on two gannets offshore, 'that we most value in our life here?'

The gannets dived, disappeared for a second or two, then reappeared, flapping in the water, gorging their fish. Then up they went majestically into the sky.

'The taste of freedom in its purest sense,' she replied.

I knew what she meant. Freedom was once governed in this country by common sense, just as behaviour was governed by conscience. Laws were then limited to guarding the framework of freedom and these laws were respected, just as the rules of behaviour were respected. Of course there were abuses, but the offenders had to risk the moral condemnation of their comrades, an intangible punishment which hurt. Today there is no such condemnation. We have become instead bemused by cynicism, and by the overwhelming mass of legislation which, although enacted in the name of freedom, is eroding it. Freedom is no longer synonymous with fair play for the conscientious, the loyal, those with pride in work well done, and the man who cherishes his chosen way of life. Instead, in this affluent age, freedom relishes the chip on the shoulder and the couldn't care less brigades, blackmail of the public by striking minorities, high wages without responsibility, obliteration of the corner shop and the small farm, and a creeping destruction of the values which aeons of time have proved to be the base upon which our inward happiness depends.

Thus when Jeannie said 'the taste of freedom in its purest sense', she was thinking as Emily Brontë was thinking when she roamed the moors above Haworth, mankind and all its chains banished from her mind; the glorious awareness that there are dimensions in living which wait to be discovered by those who are prepared to discard their man-made prejudices, open their eyes and ears, and have the patience to be quiet. Quietness is the secret. Quietness opens the door to sensitive pleasures. The noise lovers will never understand them, never know them. They may see, but they will not feel.

Such pleasures as the freedom of a Red Admiral butterfly on a sunny September afternoon, red and black patch of velvet touched with white against the pale cliff green of an ivy leaf, about to migrate across the Bay of Biscay to Spain and beyond. Young badgers on moonlit nights whimpering in play. The fragrance of a Peace rose with dew-covered petals on a June morning. A lizard motionless on a sun-baked rock camouflaged by grey lichen. Swallows saying goodbye, with see-saw flights over our small reservoir. The summer hum of a bee busy within a cup of a flower. Exquisite spider webs across rarely used paths. A chiff chaff on a prickly, white blossomed blackthorn branch proclaiming on an April morning its arrival from Africa. Grasshoppers hopping in dry summer grass as if playing games. Gales, blocked by summer leaves on trees, taking their revenge by blackening the leaves before their time is over, gales hissing and roaring when there are no leaves to check them as they rush on their way. The cottage listens, and we are warm inside. A gull calls on the roof. 'It's Philip,' I say when I look up through the glass top of the porch. Philip who has been with us for many years, and receives special treatment. 'I shouldn't,' says Jeannie, 'but here's a slice of the beef.' And she throws it up on the roof, and Philip skids down its side, and gollops the beef. Salt, sticky on my face as I walk the cliff, the wind off the sea. The donkeys competing with us as we pick black-berries. Lama pouncing during an October afternoon upon a daddy-long-legs. The earthy smell of drying bracken. The weird, beautiful cry of the curlew, the poor man's pheasant, as it flies in packs over the August countryside, heading for the Helford estuaries in the evening. Nothing to do except to watch. The timelessness of nature, yet the remorseless passing of such timelessness. Here at Minack we are lucky enough to belong to the secret beginning and the secret ending. We do not know what has happened. We are only aware what is around us has a value beyond rational explanations.

We collected the holly and lost Lama. It was the usual temporary loss when we went down the cliff. She thought it funny to hide from us, and listen to us calling against the sound of the sea below; and when at last she decided to appear from the undergrowth in which she had been tolerantly watching us, her game had not yet finished. She proceeded to tantalise us by walking very slowly up the steep path, then would pause to sniff the sea air, as if she was saying: 'I've got plenty of time even if you haven't.'

'Come on Lama, come on,' I would call, and she would look in another direction.

The game always ended in the same way. I would advance towards her, be thankful when she didn't race away, pick her up and carry her up the field. I would carry her in my arms as carefully, Jeannie has always said, as if I had been carrying the Crown jewels. This may be so. No Crown jewel, however, could make such an ill tempered whine of protest as this little black cat who was being carried up a cliff against her will. Nor was this the end of her show of independence. Once in the field, she wanted to return to the cliff. If I put her down too soon, if I was half-way up the field instead of being within sight of the cottage, her com-pact little person would dart away, heading for the cliff again. This wild, lovely cliff, where the only man-made things are the meadows Jeannie and I have created from the undergrowth, where hunted foxes can aim to reach when they run, where badgers can nose enquiringly from their setts for danger; and find none.

I kept a watch out for Oliver as we neared the cottage but there was no sign, and Lama was able to saunter up the path and into the porch without incident. The Christmas tree was in the porch. It was placed in the corner by the door on the seat-top of the cupboard where we keep our Wellington boots. It was, as usual, a small Christmas tree given us by our old friend Fred Galley, who was foreman of the wholesalers which sell our tomatoes. The gift, along with a bunch of mistletoe, was donated with customary Christmas aplomb. Jeannie had to fetch it. Jeannie willingly indulged in the customary boisterous Christmas jokes. Jeannie was kissed; Fred Galley holding the mistletoe aloft above her head as he did so. It was always a happy occasion.

The Christmas tree was carefully decorated by Jeannie and even now, long after she first played with one of the red baubles, Lama was always ready to play again. In that long ago first Christmas the tree was a big one, and it stood in a corner of the sitting room; and it was easy for her to play with the baubles. Now she had to wait until one fell off on to the floor, and when this happened, anyone who was watching was treated to a fine display of high class football. We had the usual temperamental Christmas electric candlelights . . . ten lights on, one off, all lights on, then all off. However at this moment when we arrived back with the holly and, because dusk was beginning to fall, I switched on the lights, all of them blazed. It was a pretty sight both indoors and out; and the lights shone on the green leaves of the climbing geranium that clung to the wire fastened to the old stones of the cottage outside.

'I think,' I said, 'Oliver and Ambrose ought to have their feast. Feed them now, and we won't have to bother about them for the rest of the evening.'

Jeannie had a piece of holly in her hand.

'You go and find them. I'll finish putting the holly up. Then we can feed them together.'

The John Dory had already been cooked, and it was

divided between two saucers. Delicious, fresh fish. A wonderful feast for any cat.

I had, to my surprise, no difficulty in finding them. They had already gone to bed in the flower house. I went down there where their two boxes, each full of hay, stood side by side on the flower bench; and found them together in the larger one. Silky ginger fur merged with black fur, paws around each other, two sleepy enquiring faces looking at me with strands of hay upon their heads.

'Are you ready to have a feast?' I said.

A silly question, but their look forced me to say something.

'Stay there,' I added, 'and we'll bring you one.'

But as I finished this sentence, Ambrose jumped out of the box, and ran along the bench towards where the lemon tree grows, as if the devil was chasing him. No devil chased Oliver. Oliver was relaxed, and looked at me sleepy eyed, and stayed in the box. He needed no feast to make him happy. He was happy already. Last Christmas he was in the Wren House with mud outside. This Christmas he was in the dry of the flower house, and his offspring was with him. He had no complaints. He was advancing. He had no reason to behave as if the devil was chasing him.

Nor, ostensibly, had Ambrose any reason. True he was barely three months old but already there were signs that he possessed a neurotic nature. There was a mind barrier between him and us, and although he gladly accepted our practical approaches in the cause of his comfort, he was not going to pay any rent for them. No cuddles, no games, no purrs. Ambrose was not going to conform as Monty and Lama conformed once they had come into our lives. He wanted to keep his distance. For some reason, even at this early age, he distrusted the human race.

So Jeannie, in due course, concocted an explanation for his attitude; and although practical people might say that the explanation is one of nonsense, I believe it has some substance. It is simply this. The mother of Ambrose had become obsessed over the years at the way her kittens had been taken away from her. This terrible fear had been communicated in cat language to Oliver who proposed that she should bring one of her kittens to Minack where he promised to look after it. Hence Ambrose's mysterious arrival, hence Oliver's devotion to him, hence Ambrose's inborn fear of the human race.

We never saw any sign of his mother around Minack; and although Oliver continued to disappear from time to time, it was now only for a few hours, and not for the few days which once had been the case. He behaved as if he now had a purpose in his life, and that his roaming days were over, like an erratic husband who had become a devoted father. Jeannie, with her profound knowledge of cats, said she had never known such a situation before. A tom cat who had taken charge of a kitten, who would play games with it and take it for walks, who would huddle close to it and help lick it dry after being out in the rain. Oliver loved Ambrose. There was no doubt about that.

Indeed it was Oliver's capacity to love which was our problem. He had now reached a stage when he would burst into a roaring purr whenever we came near him as he lay in one of his hay filled beds; and he would nudge his head against our outstretched fingers, and his yellow eyes would look meltingly at us. This put me in a particularly vulnerable position. Jeannie could be expected, as a chronic cat lover, to be impressed. I, on the other hand, yearned to ignore his affection, but couldn't. I was like someone who, content in the comfortable routine of his or her life, had met a potential mistress or lover. Conventionally happy at one moment, but intuitively aware at the next that the stranger you had just met was already a part of you. That, because of some alchemy, you belonged to each other. An affair which might bring a period of pleasure if you had the patience to sustain the deceptions; or a sense of frustration for many years afterwards if you hadn't.

Oliver, I realised, belonged to Minack. Here he was at peace, as far as a cat who was forbidden indoors could be at peace; and it was this acceptance of ourselves on his part which caused me increasing concern. I have never been able to consider animals as soul-less objects because I believe that animals are as sensitive as human beings, more so in fact. A human being can always throw up false defences when his ego is threatened. An animal, however, can only react with truth. Hence when Oliver purred he was expressing unadulterated pleasure. He was not deceiving. He was not behaving like a human being who calculatingly flatters in order to gain a personal advantage. On the other hand I was unpleasantly aware that, as a tom cat, he was capable of sudden and savage behaviour; and that, although he did not appear to be a very active tom, he remained a permanent threat to Lama. Lama would scent him, and bolt back to the cottage. Lama would see him in the lane, and would not dare to walk down to my office where she had spent so many hours of her life. It was a dilemma which would soon have to have a solution. We could not indefinitely continue under such tension.

We brought the saucers of John Dory down to the flower house, waved one of them in front of Oliver's nose whereupon he jumped out of his box in excitement, then put them side by side on the floor. There was no sign of Ambrose but we guessed he would soon arrive after we had left, and so we went back to the cottage to begin our own Christmas Eve evening. A quiet evening for that matter. We had a drink or two, Jeannie spent an hour wrapping up parcels in the spare room which was once the chicken house, and we both wracked our brains for pungent little verses which would accompany the presents to each other, and the presents we organised for each other from the animal and bird inhabitants of Minack. An absurd game which amused us, and with results which always proved Jeannie the more pungent.

We had dinner in the porch by the lights of the Christmas tree, and then began our wait for the ceremony of the mincepies. Of course we had no true cause to wait because the donkeys would have delightedly eaten them at any time, but we had started a tradition of waiting until a quarter of an hour before midnight, and we were determined to maintain it. The ceremony had been inspired by another tradition, the tradition that donkeys the world over go down on their knees as the clock strikes midnight on Christmas Eve, an act they are also supposed to perform at midnight before Palm Sunday. Such a tradition, I believe, is best left to the imagination. We have never set out to establish its reality because we always leave the donkeys to themselves a few minutes before midnight. We leave them in the stables quietly savouring the last of their mincepies, and although we have been tempted to watch through the window which faces the lane, we have never dared do so. We prefer fairy stories to keep their magic.

Lama meanwhile during the course of our wait had retired to bed. She had chosen the cupboard in the spare room, curling herself among my shirts, and betraying her presence by regular, gentle snores. It was a favourite place of hers, although she had other favourite places according to her mood. There was what we call the Heatpurr, for instance. The Heatpurr was a Heatstore night storage heater, and Lama greatly enjoyed lying on the shelf which covered it, especially when Jeannie had laid out newly washed garments to air. She liked also the Heatpurr in the sitting room between my desk and the window, although in this case she always curled close to it on the floor instead of lying on the shelf. Indeed for the rest of my life I will instinctively look downwards as I move from my desk to the window. For it was easy to step on Lama in the darkness of the shadow.

Soon after half past eleven I said to Jeannie it was time to prepare for the mincepie ceremony, and I was glad that it was so. Neither of us are late stayers up, and all my life I have relished nine hours' sleep. Of course quite often I wake up half-way through the night, and this period is sometimes productive of ideas; and so I console myself that I am not really wasting too much time in bed. Nevertheless it is a salutary thought that in every ten years, I have my eyes closed for nearly four of them.

'I'm ready,' said Jeannie, 'you carry the plate . . . I have the matches for the candle.'

She was standing in the porch, the Christmas tree and its lights beside her, putting on a coat. I was about to join her when she turned and looked out through the glass door into the night.

'Derek,' she said, and the tone of her voice was enough to show that something had startled her, 'come quick . . . just look outside!'

There they were, Oliver and Ambrose, faces upturned towards the lights of the Christmas tree. Two Christmas Eve outsiders, side by side, one with the look of a choirboy, the other as if he had an unbearable desire to join us. A pretty sight, though I did not admit this to Jeannie.

'Any John Dory left?' I asked without emotion.

'A little.'

'That's what they're after,' I said.

And I fussed, looking for my coat, while Jeannie went to the kitchen for the fish.

TWELVE

We never wish to go away from Minack. Sometimes I regret our lack of enterprise, and I realise that those who live in cities and noise filled streets have an advantage over us in this respect. They *have* to go away. They *have* to find places where they can recover from the tediousness of their environment. We have no need to do so because we live in surroundings we love. We are content in our compound. We do not have to say as so many have to say : 'I must get away from this cement world I live in, from the traffic and the noise, from the strain of my job and the *pressures*.'

I admit, however, that when I read the travel articles about far off places, look at the seductive advertisements, and hear of friends who have flown off to that or this corner of the world, I am sorry I have not been able to explore such places with Jeannie, for the only time we have ever been abroad together was for a month in Paris.

Yet then I reflect that the character of travel has changed since then, and since the time, just before the war, I went round the world. I was a traveller then, and a traveller was someone who was accepted by the local inhabitants as a stranger who should be given a natural welcome. Today there is no such person as a traveller. A traveller has become a tourist; and tourists the world over are assessed by the local inhabitants in terms of revenue.

On occasions, however, we do have to go away; and one such occasion loomed in front of us not long after Christmas. We were invited to stay at the newly built Berkeley Hotel in Wilton Place off Knightsbridge for its opening party, the last, probably, of the truly luxury hotels which will ever be built in London. And one reason for the invitation was, of course, Jeannie's past position in the luxury hotel world . . . her book *Meet Me At The Savoy* was the story of her life as Public Relations Officer of the Savoy Group, and her novel *Hotel Regina* was described by a BBC reviewer as 'incomparably better than Vicki Baum's *Grand Hotel*'.

Thus the years she has spent at Minack, helping to dig potatoes, weeding anemones and violets, cooking in the tiny cottage, her clothes becoming green as she tended the tomato plants, shoulders growing tired as she heaved the daffodil boxes . . . had not checked the top professional hoteliers from knowing her worth. She might live in the country but she would never adopt provincial standards. She had a sophisticated hotelier mind, and this was recognised. *Gourmet* Magazine of New York, for instance, had recognised this and had proposed she could go anywhere she liked and write for them (the Berkeley was one such place and she wrote a world-quoted article about it). But, as far as Jeannie was concerned, most important of all, her one time chief Sir Hugh Wontner, Chairman of the Savoy Group and Lord Mayor of London, appreciated her flair as well. Hence his personal invitation to attend the Berkeley opening party.

The invitation, however, posed a problem. A million pound hotel might have an opening party, but we first had to consider the welfare of Lama. Always before when we had gone away she had had no rivals esconced at Minack, and although naturally we had never liked leaving her we knew she was safe wandering around on her own with Geoffrey keeping an eye on her and shutting her up in the cottage when his working day was over. But this time she might not be safe. Geoffrey would not have the time to guard her as we guarded her. Nor was it fair to expect him to do so because one lapse on his part and she might be face to face with Oliver, or she might sniff the tom cat scent and be terrified, as we had already seen her terrified. It was an impossible project.

A decision is often postponed until circumstances force you to make one; and for weeks we had been wavering about having Oliver doctored. The time had now come when we could waver no more, and so I contacted our vet, and one morning he collected both Oliver and Ambrose, bringing them back a couple of hours later, whereupon they both buried their faces in saucers of fish. They have been content ever since.

As for Lama, she was changed by this new situation in that she soon showed no signs of fear, no signs of sniffing a tom cat around. Of course this eased our minds, though we were not so foolish as to think that they would ever be friends. When we were away Geoffrey would have to watch that they did not meet, and while Lama was out he would have to make sure that Oliver and Ambrose were secure in the greenhouse. But we believed that the threat that Oliver might ever attack her was now over. She would be vexed by his presence, and that would be all. She would no longer be scared. Indeed, and this in due course turned out to be correct, she would impose her personality upon him by her haughty demeanour. Oliver, in fact, was to be made to feel a second class citizen.

We set off for London, therefore, without qualms; and proceeded to enjoy the transfer from cottage to luxury; and it was luxury on a scale that was unusual. The Berkeley was not yet open for ordinary guests and we had, except for one other couple, the whole hotel to ourselves. Nobody else on our floor, or the floor below, or the floor above. It was as if we were Arabian oil potentates. It was as if I had had a mad dream in which Jeannie and I owned a luxury hotel in which nobody else was allowed to stay. There we were a few hours away from Lama, Oliver, Ambrose, and the donkeys which at that moment would be munching the grass in the stable meadow . . . and we could press a button, and sophisticated hotel staff would hurry to fulfil our demands because there was no one else to hurry to. It was comic.

The opening party was in the evening after we arrived. It

was scheduled to begin at six o'clock, and we decided to ask my aunt to tea beforehand. My aunt, now ninety years old, was an old friend of Lama, as some no doubt will remember. For when my aunt used to stay with us at Minack, she would try to woo Lama, although basically she was very much anti-cat. The two of them eventually came to a friendly understanding, and my aunt has always shown an endearing interest in Lama's activities.

Thus when she came to tea, she was soon to ask: 'And what about Lama?' We then explained the predicament which we were in, the divided loyalty, the mixed up emotions which occur when love is offered you when you do not want it. I found myself becoming quite unsettled until my aunt interrupted in practical fashion, saying: 'These kind of problems solve themselves.'

My aunt lived alone, and was happy doing so. She had an intense interest in all that was happening in the world whether it concerned politics, art, theatre, movies, television plays, tennis or golf. She was an admirable example of how to grow old and to remain young in heart. She was my mother's younger sister and she shared my mother's enthusiasm for life so that she, like my mother, was always loved by young people. They found her contemporary in her thinking so that they were stimulated into talking about their affairs and activities because they knew that my aunt was genuinely interested.

Jeannie has always loved her, and when the three of us are together it is advisable for me to take a back seat, and quietly listen to them prattling on about clothes, and what Jeannie's friends are doing, and all the other gossip which they exchange between them. My aunt has been a widow for many years and has never had any children of her own, a fact, she says, she has never regretted. Nor have Jeannie and I any regrets for that matter. Like my aunt we are happy in the company of children, but we have never wished to have a family of our own. Our personal lives have been complete enough to manage without additions, and had we had a family we would never have found our way to Minack.

Instead, like a countless number of conscientious parents, we would have worried about earning a sensible living until we woke up one morning and found the family life was over, and our own youthful dreams unfulfilled. Anyhow this overpopulated world can do, I believe, with more people who are happy without families.

My aunt was late in leaving after tea. We escorted her downstairs and into a taxi, then panic. I found the time had gone so fast in her company that Jeannie and I had less than half an hour to change and be ready to join the distinguished company in the ballroom; and after such a special invitation we did not want to arrive late.

We hurried back to our suite, and while Jeannie began her changing, I threw off my clothes and rushed into the bathroom for a shower . . . too hastily, too hastily. I turned on the taps, stepped into the bath and stood up. Bang! I had misjudged the height of the shower, and the top of my head had made contact with the metal spray whence cascaded the water. My predicament was obvious. Twenty minutes to go, and a cut on my head. I thereupon shut off the shower, seized a towel and wrapped it around my middle, then held my sponge under the cold tap of the basin, placed it on my head as if it was a pad of cotton wool, and walked into the bedroom.

'I've cut my head,' I said excitedly, expecting sympathy.

Jeannie took no notice. I saw she had a needle and cotton in her hand, and the black dress she was to wear lay neatly on the bed.

'I've cut my head,' I repeated. It was most unlike Jeannie not to rush to my aid in such circumstances; and the sight of me standing there with a sponge on my head should have been enough to tell her that something seriously was wrong.

She now had the needle in one hand and the cotton in the other.

'A button has come off my dress,' she said.

'Oh, my God!'

Fifteen minutes to go.

'And I can't thread the cotton through the needle . . .

144

please, please will you do it for me while I get on with my dressing . . . '

Such a moment as this, I thought, as I took the needle, was feminine indulgence . . . a button off a dress being infinitely more important than a cut head.

But I screwed up my eyes, held the cotton in my fingers, and lanced it towards the eye of the needle. I missed. I missed again. And again.

'Damn,' I said.

Then I caught a look of myself in the mirror. I was reminded of African ladies who balance pottery jugs on their heads, except that I was balancing a sponge.

'There!' I said at last and in triumph, 'I've done it!' and handed Jeannie the threaded needle.

She dropped it.

There are times when I am amazed at my patience. I, often an impatient person, can suddenly find myself so serene that a stranger meeting me at such a moment would come to the conclusion that I was constantly phlegmatic.

'Let me try again,' I said gently.

Jeannie was so impressed by my behaviour that she suddenly displayed interest in my injury. Naturally, at this stage, I laughed it off. The shock of it was over; and although the sponge was still perched on the top of my head, I sensed the worst was over. I had cut it, it had bled, but the cold water in the sponge was healing it.

Five minutes left. Needle in left hand, cotton in right, and I lunged.

'I've done it again!'

My cry of triumph echoed around the room. This new, marvellous luxury hotel might echo many cries of triumph in the years to come, but seldom one so triumphant as this. My second threading of the needle had been achieved at the first attempt.

We joined the line waiting to be received by Sir Hugh Wontner, Miss Bridget d'Oyly Carte, grand-daughter of the founder of the Savoy, and Mr Charles Fornara, general manager of the Berkeley. None of them, of course, could have guessed the domestic drama in which we had been involved as we smilingly shook hands. Nor would they have thought it funny had they known. This was their moment of triumph, the years of planning, and the first public presentation of an hotel which will for decades ahead represent the achievement of those who believe in standards, in style rather than in uniformity. It was as if we were all present at the unveiling of a genuine picture, instead of a fake.

Unfortunately for myself, the ceiling of the ballroom where the party was held was of glass, and astonishingly beautiful. As the party progressed, however, I was disturbed by the number of people who remarked to me: 'I've just seen your head up there . . . how did you cut it?'

We returned to soothing Minack; and immediately we were off the train at Penzance, Geoffrey meeting us, we were asking: 'How's Lama and the others?'

'Lama slept all the time . . . hardly came out. There was no trouble at all.'

'And the donkeys?'

'Fred hooted a lot.'

'And the gulls?'

'They cried a lot!'

Such questions and answers may appear trivial, though for us, after our glimpse of a city, they mirrored the essence of our lives. For though a glimpse of a city is a stimulating experience, it also confirms what one already knows, that the great majority of people can only tolerate the pace of their existence by worshipping instant pleasures; and that they have no time, or the patience, to take part in the gentle, subtle aspects of living. Hence, when we returned to Minack, the awareness of our luck in having such a home had once again been sharpened.

We had come back, however, to a warm spring, and we do not like warm springs. The sun beat down on the daffodil beds as if it had mistaken March for June, and instead of the daffodils remaining in bud as the market demanded, they popped uncontrollably into bloom. All over Cornwall they were popping into bloom.

'Wonderful weather we're having,' someone would say to me.

'It's ghastly,' I would puzzle them in replying.

Jeannie and I would be up at dawn and out in the meadows picking, catching the blooms before the sun, bent double, hastening up the rows, filling the baskets which waited at either end. Why did we enjoy this simple, automatic task? Why did we feel that something positive was being achieved? An actuary would ridicule us. The computer, he would say, proves that you are wasting your time. Find something else to do.

There was a reward, though, in being out there with the wind coming in from the sea, and gulls waking up, floating into the sky from the rocks, and catching sight of a vixen loping her way back across Fred's field towards her earth in the cliff; and the space and silence around us. Sometimes, while Lama lay curled on our bed continuing her sleep, we would be joined by Oliver and Ambrose, and as the sun rose above the Lizard they would play games among the daffodils.

Ambrose, whose first experience of daffodils it was, found it hugely amusing to hide among the green stems, then sneak towards Oliver who was sauntering along a gap between two beds . . . and playfully pounce. There was also another antic which was funny to watch. The two of them would walk together within the rows so that their bodies were hidden, and only the tops of their tails were seen, like the periscopes of two submarines. Then suddenly they would start to play, chasing each other, and the top of their tails would change from being dignified periscopes into looking like flags being waved excitedly; and the sight was amusing enough for us to say whenever they appeared in those early mornings: 'The flag wavers have arrived!'

But early morning picking, however pleasurable, however worthy in intent, has to face reality sooner or later; and for three days in succession we received warnings that we were, as the imaginary actuary had said, wasting our time. The warnings were scrawled on the invoice notes from our Covent Garden salesman . . . 'daffs arriving too open', they said. Yet these were the daffs we had picked in the dawn light before the sun had touched them and broken their buds. We had packed them in tight bud. I had driven them to Penzance station confident we were sending them away in ideal market condition, yet they had arrived at Covent Garden too open . . . because daffodil boxes in warm weather generate heat as they travel, crammed one on top of each other in the truck; and our early morning efforts to beat the sun were therefore valueless.

Indeed so valueless that the morning post one day brought an invoice with the words : 'No sale'.

Never in all the years we had been sending flowers to Covent Garden had this happened before.

'No sale,' I shrieked in anger to Jeannie and Geoffrey after opening the envelope. And if they didn't shriek back in sound, their looks suggested they were wishing to do so.

We didn't send any daffodils away again after that. We didn't even send the daffodils we had picked that early morning, and which Jeannie had already packed and Geoffrey had tied and labelled. They stood in their boxes on the long bench, a tangible demonstration of wasted effort.

'Never mind,' said Jeannie, 'they'll give pleasure to the hospital.' And later in the day the matron and her staff at the Penzance Hospital had the formidable task of finding vases for dozens of bunches of daffodils.

The flower season was over, and the sun continued to shine as in high summer, and we had time again on our hands.

THIRTEEN

Jeannie's sister Barbara came to stay with us in May from her home at Coton-in-the-Clay near Derby. She had always referred to Lama as the Princess; and when she arrived on this occasion she exclaimed that she had never seen the Princess look so pretty. It was easy to agree. The Princess was plump, her coat glossy like a ripe blackberry, and her fat tail made a mockery of the object that belonged to Oliver. Her little face, except for the drooping white whiskers, looked as young as a kitten; and she was often as playful. I would suddenly spy her tapping a paw at a feather which had come from one of the gulls on the roof, or I would watch her indoors chasing a demon under a rug, pushing her head underneath in an effort to catch it. She was still young, it seemed, and there was no sign of the years she had been with us since that day she arrived at the door in a storm. Except that Barbara saw one, though it was a sign which, at the time, I preferred to ignore.

Often, when she settled on my lap after breakfast, lunch or dinner, pinning me down in a corner of the sofa until the time came when she decided to release me, I would make use of the situation by combing her. The comb was kept in the drawer of the small Regency table on the left of the sofa, and I would twist my body into contortions so that I could extract the comb from the drawer without disturbing the Princess on my lap.

I would then gently begin my task. First a comb along the ridge of the back, then another between the ears but with such care that she still proceeded to look sleepily at Jeannie in the chair opposite; and next a bolder comb in the thicker fur regions of her side, a move which if successful, reaped a harvest of silky, rich down; and this I would sometimes keep, putting it in a box decorated with sea shells, because I thought that one day I would want a tangible memory of her. I had done the same when I used to comb Monty, and his is still there in a small *pot-pourri* bowl of Swansea china which stands on top of the bookshelves. Thus I would sit in my corner delicately performing my task until Lama told me she had had enough by crossly attacking the comb. I would immediately stop.

The cross attacks, however, had recently become more frequent. She showed an increasing dislike of my combing the denser parts of her fur, and the reason was easy to understand, for although the surface of her coat appeared to be in perfect condition, underneath it was becoming matted. This was a sign of her age that Barbara pointed out to me.

Others pointed it out to me in another way. Visitors who made remarks like :

'Lama's getting on, isn't she?'

'Have you *still* got Lama?'

'She's a good age.'

Age, age, age. The British are besotted about age. If a woman walks down a street, slips on a banana peel, falls and breaks her leg, be sure the press will begin the report : 'Fifty-five-year-old Mrs So-and-So . . . ' Age had to be tagged on to any news. It's a ritual. It had become a ritual to ask Lama's age . . . and I found myself going back over the years and remembering the same questions being asked about Monty. Nothing had changed. The same dismay at the questions, the same sadness, the same stifled awareness that I was blinding myself to the truth. Yes, I knew that Lama was coming to the end of her time and that she would become a black comma in my memory, but I did not want to be reminded of this by such questions. I could touch her now, pick her up, listen to her purr, and I did not want to be told that these subtle pleasures would one day be only a dream.

Such moments of depression, however, were only a shallow layer on the happiness of that summer. There was, for instance, the amusement, and confusion, caused by Oliver and Ambrose. We had already become accustomed to those who excitedly exclaimed: We saw Lama as we were coming up the lane!' . . . when, in fact, they had seen Oliver. But Ambrose had never been called Monty until a friend whom we had not seen for many years was startled by the sight of him on the inside window-sill of the barn.

'I thought Monty was dead!'

'So he is . . . years ago.'

'I must have just seen his ghost!'

It has often seemed to me that many people, especially those who are leaders of a country, of a community, or of a cause, treat logic as a kind of lifebelt. They are desperately anxious to believe that they are masters of their own destinies, and that they can control the paths of these destinies by neat planning. Thus logic, backed up by elaborately documented facts and figures, provides the basis of any report on any subject you can name; and the imponderables are ignored because they are too mysterious to contemplate.

The imponderables, in this case, were represented by Oliver and Ambrose. How can anyone, however astute and logical in their thinking, explain the arrival at Minack of two wild, uninvited cats which were the doubles of the only two cats I have ever known?

Sensible people, no doubt, might explain it away by saying that it was a coincidence, and no more. Sensible people are inclined to ignore the existence of those unseen, untouchable, extra-sensory forces which push us this way and that during the course of our lives; and this is because the Western world believes itself so civilised that to consider magic as a reality is beneath its dignity. Yet many of us know of incidents that have no rational explanation.

A parson told me the other day of a little girl in his parish of whom he was particularly fond, who was found unconscious by her parents one morning. She had shown no previous symptoms, and when she reached hospital doctors were unable to diagnose the cause of her illness. Two days later hope for her life was given up; and the parents asked the parson to hurry to the hospital and give her a blessing. Just before he set off, the parson rang up a healer who was a friend of his, and told him of his mission. An hour later he reached the hospital only to be greeted with the news that the child, who had never regained consciousness, was not expected to live more than a few minutes. He hurried to the ward, and stood by the girl's bed, then quietly said: 'Who is here, Jill? Who is here?' There was stillness for a moment, then the girl stirred, and to the astonishment of everyone murmured: 'It's you, Father.' From that instant the recovery began, and a month or so later she was riding her pony again in the fields near her home. Was it prayer, the healer, or magic which achieved this?

As for my own experience in these mysterious matters, one incident which sticks in my mind concerns the one and only time I have had my hand read by a palmist. I was on a steamer sailing from Sydney to Hong Kong when one of my fellow passengers, a burly engineer on his way to a job in Hong Kong dockyard, offered to tell me my fortune, saying that he had once studied with Cheiro, a renowned palmist. So there I was on deck one balmy evening, the steamer sailing through the Aragura Sea, with my hands held out in front of me . . . and the engineer telling me that I would marry a slender, dark haired girl whose initials were J.E. Five years later I was walking up the aisle of Richmond Church with Jean Everald Nicol.

Anyhow, whatever the explanation for the arrival of Oliver and Ambrose, I the anti-cat man was now besieged by three cats; and I was endlessly on guard. Lama, although she was no longer frightened by Oliver, understandably disliked his presence; and so we continued to do our best to keep them apart. Thus I was perpetually saying: 'No sign of Oliver, Lama can go out.' Or: 'Keep Lama in. Oliver is around the corner.' As for Ambrose, he continued to be elusive, *maddeningly* elusive.

'Come here, Ambrose,' I would call, waggling a finger towards him.

Or:

'I have something for you, Ambrose,' Jeannie would say, holding a saucer of fish in one hand while hoping to stroke him with the other.

Not a chance.

'Ambrose,' I would remark sternly, 'pay your rent!'

His markings, month by month, became more beautiful, lines of autumn bracken colours with shapes which reminded me of currents on a quiet sea. True that at times his head, because of his youth, looked scraggy, even his body sometimes looked scraggy, but suddenly for some reason like the change of light or of mood, he looked his potential. This was going to be a champion cat, just like Monty. Beautiful to look at, and highly intelligent though still viewing the human race, and ourselves, despite all that we were wanting to offer, with suspicion.

The relationship between him and Lama developed into a quiet understanding so that I would catch sight of them side by side at Monty's Leap, sipping from the trickle of the summer stream; and when they had finished they would walk back together. Of course Ambrose would not dare to take any advantage of her. He recognised that she was the Queen. Affection he could offer, but no question of taking liberties.

Oliver, meanwhile, was becoming benign. He was still the outsider, longing to be the insider, and sometimes he took physical steps to achieve his aim. We had this wire framed contraption, first used to prevent Monty from jumping out of the bedroom window at night, which we still erected to stop Lama from doing the same. It was an insecurely fixed, clumsy contraption, but firm enough to achieve its purpose. But one night I was woken from a deep sleep by a terrible battering noise at the window, followed by a crash on the floor, then a thump. Oliver, from the outside, had knocked down the contraption, and jumped on the bed.

Jeannie was half awake.

'What's happened? What's happened?'

She spoke in that half-hysterical fashion that half-awake people are inclined to do.

'Keep calm,' I hissed, 'leave it to me. It's an emergency.'

An emergency indeed. Oliver had crawled up to me on my left side, roaring out purrs like the sound of a low flying piston-engined aircraft, while on my right side lay Lama.

'Don't wake her,' I hissed again, 'hold her gently, and I'll deal with Oliver.'

'You're panicking.'

'Of course I'm panicking . . . the two of them within a foot of each other, and one roaring his head off an inch from my face.'

I now seized Oliver firmly in my hands, got out of bed, carried him to the sitting room door, opened it, then opened the porch door into the little garden, and dumped him there. I went back to bed.

'A bit cruel, weren't you?'

'Heavens,' I answered, 'what else could I do?'

Not a movement from Lama. She was still curled on the bed, making the clickety-click noise which was peculiar to her when she was sleeping.

'I just think it was a bit hard on him,' said Jeannie sleepily, adding, 'he only wants to be loved.'

'Oh Jeannie, you do sometimes say such silly things.'

'Shut up, I'm just going off.'

I myself didn't go off for an hour or more. I lay awake wondering what Oliver was thinking, and how he was spending the night. Back sharing a straw-filled box with Ambrose, I guessed.

The donkeys viewed Oliver and Ambrose with tolerant amusement. Oliver, they realised, was like Lama, possessing a middle-aged seriousness which forbade any prospect of playing silly games. Nevertheless they would sometimes try. If Oliver was in sight as we led the two of them from the stable meadow up past the cottage, one of them would be

154

sure to advance head down, like a dog following a scent, and try to pull towards him. Oliver, of course, would skedaddle away; and Penny or Fred, whichever it was, would take a bite at the escallonia instead.

Ambrose was a different matter. Ambrose provoked them, especially Fred. Ambrose was like a saucy small boy who taunted his friends to attack him, then ran away before they were able to do so. Ambrose courted danger. Ambrose would find Fred munching grass in the donkey field above the cottage, and proceed to stalk him. This was a dangerous form of Russian roulette because Fred was often in the middle of the field, so that the nearer Ambrose crept the further he had to run to escape. Perhaps this was Ambrose's deliberate purpose, to experience the sheer thrill of being chased a hundred yards by a donkey. It certainly gave Fred pleasure, it was bliss chasing Ambrose at speed across a field.

Thus there were three cat lives running parallel to each other at Minack that summer. Ambrose, of course, was the most innocent, the years of adventure ahead of him, and the fun, and idiotic predicaments. Oliver, understandably, was bewildered as to what more he had to do to become acceptable . . . choosing to come back in the first place, the cold nights in the Wren House and on branches of gorse when his house was flooded, the efforts to show his affection, the wondrous production by him that Sunday October morning of the double of Monty, his gentle insistence that all he wanted from us was to be loved . . . it wasn't difficult to understand why he was puzzled that we didn't allow him to become a natural part of our life. Yet he had time on his side. He could wait. He could pursue a policy of quietly infiltrating into our lives because he had the edge on Lama. He was younger. He might be made to feel, by our manner towards him, that he was a second class citizen, but he was prepared to put up with it. He had Ambrose, in any case, as a companion. He wasn't lonely.

Lama, meanwhile, spent more and more of her time in sleep. She would curl herself in her favourite places, on the carpet beside my desk close to the storage heater, or she would lie on the newly washed clothes airing on top of the storage heater in the spare bedroom, or she would settle herself in the dark of the cupboard among my shirts. Not that she showed any serious signs of her age. Her appetite was as good as ever, and she still loved her walks, the walk to the cliff especially.

I remember one hot, early September morning, and Jeannie and I decided to take time off, and to go down to the rocks to bathe; and we hadn't walked a dozen yards down the path towards Fred's field when to our surprise Lama rushed past us, then suddenly stopped, and looked back at us. This was the old game of chase and stop which we knew so well. A spontaneous gesture of pleasure and excitement.

'I didn't really want her to come,' I said.

'Why ever not?'

'I wanted to lie on the rocks and bathe,' I said, 'I wanted to be on my own without bothering about Lama.'

'You old misery.'

I accepted that. I was an old misery not to be happy that Lama had chosen to come with us. But I was right about having to bother about her. For the path wending its way down through the daffodil meadows became steeper when it neared the rocks, and at that point Lama would always stop. She would not walk on the rocks. Hence when we wanted to bathe, one of us had always to stay with her, or otherwise she would join the gulls' cries with her miaows.

That September morning I let Jeannie go ahead with her bathe, while I stayed behind with Lama, lying on the same spot as when she warned me that an adder was about to attack me. She sat on my tummy purring; and I lay there with that sound in my ears and the sound of the sea caressing the rocks, a gull or two soulfully calling, and the poignant trilling of oyster catchers over to my left below Carn Barges. A moment of great happiness, complete, breeding no greedy wish for something better. This was the kind of moment for which men and women, in old-fashioned wars, were ready to die for, believing that the simple, basic pleasures offered the key to happiness. A kind of moment which by-passed the sophisticated theories which try to govern our lives today.

Dear Lama, I still can hear her purring.

FOURTEEN

'Can we see Lama?'

Another spring.

'I'm afraid ...'

Another summer.

'We've come a long way to take a photograph of Lama.'

'I'm sorry but ...'

Another autumn.

'Is that Lama?'

'No ... I'll try to explain.'

'What *did* happen to her?'

'She died on March 3rd. Just faded away. Nothing that anyone could have done.'

'We heard *Lama* read on the radio in January.'

'I recorded it, recorded her purr before each instalment too. She was all right then, it was easy to make her purr.'

'She had a wonderful life.'

'Yes.'

'So she came to you in daffodil time, and left in daffodil time.'

'Yes.'

'A strange coincidence.'

'As strange as something that happened the evening of the day she died.'

'What was that?'

Sometimes I answered this question. Sometimes I changed the subject. It depended upon whether I thought the listener would be in tune with the magical combination of circumstances which took place that evening.

A gale began to blow in from the sea in late afternoon, and by nightfall a storm was raging around the cottage, the same storm it seemed to me, as that night when Lama first cried at the door; and suddenly I heard the cry again.

I left my chair and went over to the door, and when I opened it the light shone on Oliver and Ambrose, waiting, side by side in the wind and the rain.

A black cat, and one the colour of autumn bracken. As if Lama and Monty had returned to Minack.

A Selection of Bestsellers from Sphere Books

Fiction

SHARKY'S MACHINE	William Diehl	£1.50p ☐
THE GLENDOWER LEGACY	Thomas Gifford	£1.25p ☐
WOMAN OF FURY	Constance Gluyas	£1.40p ☐
BAAL	Robert McCammon	95p ☐
SEASON OF PASSION	Danielle Steel	£1.25p ☐

Film and TV tie-ins

THE PROFESSIONALS 5: BLIND RUN	Ken Blake	85p ☐
THE PROFESSIONALS 6: FALL GIRL	Ken Blake	85p ☐
THE PROFESSIONALS 7: HIDING TO NOTHING	Ken Blake	85p ☐
THE PROFESSIONALS 8: DEAD RECKONING	Ken Blake	85p ☐
THE PROMISE	Danielle Steel	95p ☐

Non-Fiction

SECRETS OF OUR SPACESHIP MOON	Don Wilson	£1.10p ☐
ARISTOTLE ONASSIS	Nicholas Fraser, Philip Jackson, Mark Ottaway & Lewis Chester	£1.60p ☐
SECRETS OF LOST ATLAND	Robert Scrutton	£1.50p ☐

All Sphere books are available at your local bookshop or newsagent, or can be ordered direct from the publisher. Just tick the titles you want and fill in the form below.

Name ....

Address ....

....

Write to Sphere Books, Cash Sales Department, P.O. Box 11, Falmouth, Cornwall TR10 9EN.

Please enclose cheque or postal order to the value of the cover price plus:

UK: 25p for the first book plus 10p per copy for each additional book ordered to a maximum charge of £1.05.

OVERSEAS: 40p for the first book and 12p for each additional book.

B.F.P.O. and EIRE: 25p for the first book plus 10p per copy for the next 8 books, thereafter 5p per book.

Sphere Books reserve the right to show new retail prices on covers which may differ from those previously advertised in the text or elsewhere, and to increase postal rates in accordance with the GPO.

(12:79)